Kenneth and Valerie McLeish

CRUCIAL
CLASSICS

How to Enjoy the Best Music in the World

M

MACMILLAN

LONDON

First published 1994 by Macmillan Limited
a division of Pan Macmillan Publishers Limited
Cavaye Place London SW10 9PG
and Basingstoke

Associated companies throughout the world

ISBN 0 333 63100 5

1 3 5 7 9 8 6 4 2

A CIP catalogue record for this book is available from the British Library.

Typeset in Great Britain by Spottiswoode Ballantyne, Colchester, Essex.
Printed and Bound in Great Britain by Cox & Wyman Ltd, Reading, Berkshire

CRUCIAL CLASSICS

Kenneth McLeish is the author of over eighty books, including the *Bloomsbury Good Reading Guide*. He is a busy playwright and theatre translator, and was one of the first presenters on BBC Radio 3's afternoon classic-music show, *Mainly for Pleasure*. His hobbies are gardening and comedy films.

Valerie McLeish taught music, and worked backstage for Focus Opera Group of London. With her husband, she has written over a dozen books. She plays euphonium in a local brass band and is also its chairman. Her hobbies are gardening and cooking.

CONTENTS

HOW TO USE THIS BOOK

This book offers a fair helping of the cream of classical music. We made our selection from the whole range, from the seventeenth century to just before the twenty-first, from single movements to whole operas, from minuets to symphonies.

The works are ordered alphabetically by composer. This makes them easy to find, but it doesn't mean that you should start at A and work your way through to W (though one of our sons did that with his tape collection and found that it worked extremely well). We haven't tried to give a comprehensive view of each composer's life or output, but have suggested some of his best or most enjoyable music – or, wherever possible, both. (By chance, all the composers are masculine.) We've explained something of the background to each main piece, and have tried to describe the effect the music makes. A Now TRY section after each work suggests follow-up listening, and pieces in similar mood by the same composer and others.

Scattered through the book are more general sections, on Ballet, Chamber Music, Concertos, Early Music, the History of Classical Music, Opera, Orchestral Music, Overtures, Singing, String Orchestra and Symphonies. These have suggestions of their own, and also lead to the main composer pages in the book. There are three further sections. Start Here is above all for people new to classical music, Lollipops lists some of the most succulent music in the repertoire, and ... And Don't Forget ... is about some of our own favourites, or works we couldn't squeeze in elsewhere.

Lastly, the Index lists every composer and every work mentioned. Indexes are always at the back of books, but in fact they're often the most useful entry point. But how you find your way into classical music isn't as important as what you get out of it. It's given us years of pleasure, and we hope it does the same for you. Happy listening!

Kenneth and Valerie McLeish
Spalding, 1994

START HERE

Until recording was invented about a hundred years ago, getting into classical music was no problem. Someone put on a concert, you went to listen, and hey presto! Your choice of music was made for you.

The arrival of recording changed all that. Ordinary music-lovers can now assemble concerts to suit themselves, at home, of any kind of music they choose. Tens of thousands of works are available, all clamouring for attention. The problem is like the dilemma of a starving man or woman in a supermarket: where to start.

For most of us, the first experience is usually hearing an attractive piece on the radio, on one of the stations devoted to classical music or as part of the mixture on other channels. A classical piece might be the background to an advertisement: Orff's *Carmina Burana*, for example, once advertised male deodorant; Bach's *Air on the G String* recommended the tranquillity brought by a particular brand of small cigar; Rossini's *Barber of Seville* music memorably accompanied shots of robots building cars. Classical pieces are often used as theme music for films, TV and radio series, and for sporting events: Wagner's 'Ride of the Valkyries' (*Apocalypse Now*); Mozart's *Eine Kleine Nachtmusik* (*Brain of Britain*); Chopin's *Minute Waltz* (*Just a Minute*); Sousa's *Liberty Bell* (*Monty Python's Flying Circus*); Copland's *Fanfare for the Common Man* (theme of the Olympics); Puccini's 'Nessun dorma' (sung by Pavarotti for the 1990 World Cup).

Pieces of this kind are often collected on compilation

discs or tapes, and the associations (such as adverts) are mentioned. So even if you don't know the music's name you can find the piece you want. Once you *do* know the name, it's easy to go to record shops or the dozens of guidebooks, catalogues and other lists in libraries, to follow up any particular kind of music you like, any composer, or any performer – Nigel Kennedy on violin, James Galway on flute, the glorious voices of Kiri Te Kanawa or José Carreras.

It's at about this point, we think, that fatigue sets in. As with most kinds of music, people tend to fix on a few favourite artists or styles, and ignore the rest. Classical music, however, is different from most other kinds, simply because so much more is available. It's almost inexhaustible; exploration is guaranteed to turn up riches. The two of us have been classical music fans all our lives, and we still find new composers and new works, almost every week.

That, perhaps, is where books like this come in. If you start with a name that catches your eye or a work whose sound you like, and follow up our suggestions one by one (but leaving aside any you don't enjoy – this isn't a school textbook; nothing is compulsory), you should end up experiencing music of dozens of different kinds by over four hundred composers. It's a drop in the ocean, but it's a start.

While we were planning this book, we wrote down a list of twenty pieces *we* would include on a compilation tape or CD: immediately familiar, attractive works, like tasters in a food shop. (It's on page xi.) If you're entirely new to classical music and want a toe-hold, these are the pieces we recommend. All have entries later in the book – those asterisked are under the composer's name, the Copland is on page 106.

Recordings differ in quality and price. Experienced

listeners often have favourite artists, or prefer recordings of a particular type or vintage. One of the joys of classical music is its huge variety. We recommend newcomers not to bother about any of this. Go for the music first – if you like it, *that's* the moment to start browsing in libraries, record shops and guidebooks. For the time being, please start here.

*Albinoni, Adagio
*Bach, *Air on the G String*
*Bernstein, *West Side Story* (try 'Maria')
*Bizet, *Carmen* (try 'Toreador's Song')
*Borodin, *Polovtsian Dances*, from *Prince Igor*
Copland, *Fanfare for the Common Man*
*Delibes, 'Flower Duet' from *Lakmé*
*Dvořák, Symphony No. 9, 'New World' (slow movement)
*Fauré, *Requiem*
*Gershwin, *Porgy and Bess* (try 'Summertime')
*Handel, *Messiah* (try the 'Hallelujah' Chorus)
*Khachaturian, *Spartacus* (try the Adagio)
*Orff, *Carmina Burana* (first movement)
*Puccini, *Turandot* (try 'Nessun dorma')
*Rachmaninov, Piano Concerto No. 2 (first movement)
*Ravel, *Boléro*
*Rossini, Overture to *William Tell*
*Johann Strauss, *The Blue Danube*
*Tchaikovsky, *1812* Overture
*Vivaldi, *The Four Seasons* (try 'Spring')
*Wagner, 'Ride of the Valkyries'

ALBINONI
Adagio

This short piece brought its composer a fortune, but absolutely no fame at all. The composer in question was not in fact Albinoni, but the musical scholar Remo Giazotto, who lived and worked some two hundred years after Albinoni's death, by which time Albinoni was a forgotten figure from an unpopular period of the classical-music repertory.

Using only a scrap of tune for bass instruments, Giazotto supplied harmony and melody, published the result and thought no more about it. Years later, the Baroque period zoomed unexpectedly back into favour, and this piece was taken up and played everywhere. Over Albinoni's bass line, many times repeated, the other instruments weave peaceful, overlapping patterns, like water rippling against a shore on a summer day. Albinoni gets the credit; Giazotto got the money; we get music to ease the heart.

ALBINONI   Tomaso Albinoni (1671–1751), though shadowy today, was one of the most respected Venetian composers of his day. He wrote over eighty operas, as well as dozens of concertos, sonatas and church pieces. Interestingly, in view of what happened to the *Adagio*, scraps of his music were regularly reworked by other people – including even Bach, who arranged several of his concertos and 'borrowed' bass lines, just as Giazotto was to do centuries later.

MUSIC IN VENICE   In Albinoni's day, Venice was one
of the most musical cities in Europe. Each of its churches
(over a hundred) required new, live music every holy day
throughout the year. Musical evenings were a favourite
pastime, and owners of the palaces along the Grand Canal,
especially, vied with each other to sponsor the most
astounding, ear-catching novelties. Half a dozen opera
houses each mounted six or more new pieces every year.
There were music academies, and music featured in school
education. A talented composer, willing to provide what
patrons wanted, could make a handsome living without
ever travelling beyond the city boundaries.

NOW TRY   Good short follow-ups to the *Adagio*:
Pachelbel, *Canon*. Handel, 'Largo' (from *Serse*). Bach, 'Jesu,
Joy of Man's Desiring'. Works 100 per cent by Albinoni:
any of his short oboe concertos (a kind of music he
pioneered in Italy); any of his *concerti grossi*. Follow-ups:
Vivaldi, 'Spring' (from *The Four Seasons*); Handel, Organ
Concerto 'The Cuckoo and the Nightingale'; Bellini, Oboe
Concerto.

BACH
Air on the G String

Whenever advertisers want music to suggest total relaxation
and people utterly at peace with the world, they reach for
this air. We almost need a special effort of will to listen to it
as music, for its own sake, without our minds wandering to
the products it advertises – but that's hardly Bach's fault.

Bach called the piece just 'Air'. 'On the G string' was
added later, when the tune was arranged to be played all on
one string, as a stunt. (This is not done today.) It is the

second movement of Bach's Suite No. 3 for orchestra, and provides three minutes of tranquillity in the middle of bustling dance movements.

The music is in three layers. Lowest is a 'walking bass': a steady tread of notes, moving the music on calmly but purposefully. The middle layer is a shimmer of harmony, gluing the sound together. The top layer is a violin tune, long-held notes with patterns of shorter notes leading from each one to the next, as if someone were moving from hold to hold on a mountainside, sure-footed and utterly in control.

ORCHESTRAL SUITES   Dance-music suites were a popular orchestral entertainment of Bach's time: Bach himself wrote four of them. They start with intricate first movements, followed by dances in such favourite forms of the time as gavotte, minuet and jig.

BACH   Johann Sebastian Bach (1685–1750) was trained for music from boyhood, learning to play several instruments before becoming a keyboard virtuoso. He worked as a church organist until he was twenty-seven, then spent five years as music director to the court of the Prince of Cöthen, and from 1723 to his death was music director of St Thomas's Church in Leipzig. While in Cöthen Bach specialized in orchestral music (he composed the Suites during this period) in Leipzig he wrote church music – and all his life he composed for his own cherished instruments, organ and harpsichord. He was a workaholic, sustained by devout Lutheran faith, a (crowded) family life, his beloved pipe (to which he once wrote a poem) and enormous quantities of coffee.

NOW TRY   Bach, 'Jesu, Joy of Man's Desiring'; 'Sheep May
Safely Graze'; orchestral suites (starting with No. 2, for flute
and strings, rather than with No. 3). Albinoni, *Adagio*.
Bach–Gounod, 'Ave Maria'. Handel, 'Where'er You Walk'
from *Semele*.

BACH
Brandenburg Concerto No. 2

Eighteenth-century trumpets were simple instruments,
little more complicated than bugles, and could play only a
handful of notes. Composers used those notes for maximum
effect, but sparingly, so that if trumpeters worked for more
than a few minutes in each hour of music, they thought
themselves hard done by.

This concerto is different. As well as string orchestra, it
stars four soloists: violin, oboe, recorder – and high trumpet.
Bach makes no concessions, treating the trumpet as if it
were as easy to play as any other instrument. The effect, for
the player, is like expecting a quiet stroll and finding
yourself blindfold on a tightrope. For the audience, the
results can be a musical feat as thrilling as any circus trick.

There are three short movements: fast, slow, fast. Bach
lets the trumpeter sit out the second movement, resting his
or her lip, but otherwise highlights the instrument, giving
it the best tunes and making it lead the band.

THE BRANDENBURG CONCERTOS   Bach wrote these
concertos in 1712 for the court orchestra of the Margrave
(Count) of Brandenburg. As well as No. 2, three other
concertos set groups of soloists against the string orchestra:
horns and flute (No. 1), recorders and violin (No. 4), flute,

harpsichord and violin (No. 5). Nos 3 and 6 are for strings alone, giving the whole orchestral group a chance to shine.

THE BACH FAMILY Bach belonged to an amazing musical dynasty: from the sixteenth to nineteenth centuries more than sixty Bachs earned their living as town, church and court musicians in central Germany. Johann Sebastian was immensely proud of this, even writing a pamphlet about his relatives. He was the youngest of eight children, and grew up to father nineteen children of his own – or possibly twenty or twenty-one (reference books disagree). All the males of the family were trained in music, and all the females were expected to marry musicians. There have been dynasties in other professions, and dynasties of one sort or another in music – but few, if any, have ever rivalled the Bachs.

NOW TRY Bach, Brandenburg Concertos Nos 3 and 4. Handel, Concerto Grosso Op. 3 No. 1. Telemann, Concerto in E minor for recorder, flute and strings.

BACH
Toccata and Fugue in D minor

Few organ pieces are better known than this. Whenever organists appear in films – from Captain Nemo in *Twenty Thousand Leagues Under the Sea* to mad Count Dracula in his castle – it is this that they play. It was featured (in a sumptuous orchestral arrangement) in Disney's *Fantasia*. There can be few people who don't know its opening notes, and it continues and finishes just as strikingly as it begins.

A toccata is a virtuoso show-piece, and this is no exception. It is a storm of fast notes: scales, arpeggios, swooping up and down the organ keyboards and being caught each time just as they seem about to slip off the end. The main melody of the fugue (see page 230) chugs – there's no other word for it – obsessively to and from the same endlessly repeated note. (In live performances, when this melody comes on the pedals, the player's feet work up and down as if he or she were doing floor exercises.) In both toccata and fugue, the music seems every so often to freeze momentarily into huge blocks of sound, filling the building and shaking the windows, before melting again into Bach's favourite trills and runs.

BACH AND THE ORGAN   In Bach's day organists were stars, and people crowded to hear them. Bach himself often made two- or three-day journeys (on foot) to hear outstanding rivals. This Toccata and Fugue is the kind of music he himself was famous for. One admirer wrote that anyone who thought that the full, fat sound he produced was the result of magic was a fool. It was done practically: he used not only his feet and hands to play the keys, but also a stick held in his teeth. Bach retorted testily that he had the same number of fingers and toes as anyone else, and if anyone wanted to make the same sounds as he did, all they had to do was buy his music and practise it.

NOW TRY   Bach, Fugue à la gigue; 'St Anne' Fugue (on the hymn tune often sung to 'O God Our Help in Ages Past'; Trio Sonata No. 5. Widor, Toccata from Organ Symphony No. 5; Lefébure-Wély, Sortie in B flat.

BACH
Concerto in C minor for Violin and Oboe

While Bach was in his twenties he was music director for Prince Leopold of Cöthen, who kept an orchestra and loved the latest, Italian, fashions in music. These were the kind of concertos written by Vivaldi and Albinoni, and Bach dutifully studied them, learned their secrets, and then produced dazzling concertos of his own.

The Prince seems to have enjoyed hearing the same works played by different soloists. Bach regularly rearranged his concertos for different instruments. This one, for example, appeared for violin, oboe and orchestra, then for two violins, then for two harpsichords. (The two-violin version is lost, but the two-harpsichord one survives.)

The concerto is in three parts. The outside movements are brisk, muscular workouts, in which everyone shares the excitement, and the soloists provide less of a virtuoso display than a sound-contrast to the orchestra. The middle movement is slow. Over plucked-string accompaniment, the soloists play long-breathed, soulful melodies that twine round one another like lovers.

BACH'S MUSIC Bach was an expert in counterpoint. Music can be written either vertically (tune on top, accompaniment underneath) or horizontally (as a set of 'lines' which are of equal importance but blend to make an intellectually satisfying whole). This horizontal style is counterpoint, and Bach uses it incessantly. (He was especially good at fugue, the most demanding contrapuntal style of all.) But he also wrote expansive, emotionally packed melodies, tunes which speak to heart as well as head. The combination of intellectual dexterity and emotional 'pull' gives his music a sound quality few other composers have equalled.

THE MASTER Like many composers, Bach found discordant sounds almost physically painful. He once walked into a room where someone was playing the harpsichord, and the man leapt up hastily, playing a jangling discord as he did so. Bach frowned, strode to the instrument, played the discord again, and followed it by new chords of his own which resolved it into mellow concord. Only then, relaxed and beaming, did he do as etiquette demanded, bowing to his aristocratic host and hostess.

NOW TRY Bach, Concerto in D minor for two violins; Harpsichord Concerto in F minor (particularly beautiful slow movement). Albinoni, Concerto in D for two oboes. Telemann, Concerto in A minor for recorder and viola da gamba.

BACH
St Matthew Passion

This Passion was written for church performance on Good Friday. Bach sets the story, from Matthew's Gospel, of Christ's arrest, trial and execution. A narrator (tenor solo) sings Matthew's text; other voices take such parts as Christ or Pilate; the choir plays the crowd. (Their cry of 'Crucify him!' is particularly vivid.) The choir also takes the part of devout Christian believers, reacting to events with heartfelt sorrow and devotion. Every few minutes they sing a hymn to a well-known tune.

In a church, the effect can be overwhelming. But Bach's music is so powerful that even if you hear the Passion in the concert hall, even if you have no Christian belief, even if you don't speak German, you will be moved and exalted. Part of its effect is the experience of hearing it with other people; records diminish this, and sampling is recommended. (Good single pieces are the opening chorus – unflurried choral counterpoint over turbulent orchestral sounds – and the beautiful aria 'Erbarme dich, mein Gott', 'Have mercy, Lord', for alto soloist, solo violin and orchestra.)

MASSES, OPERAS AND PASSIONS   In Catholic Europe, the Mass was the main eighteenth-century church service: austere, devotional, tending to dominate the music which accompanied it. The most colourful form of vocal music was opera. In Protestant Europe there were no masses, opera was frowned on, and composers developed the Passion as a way of filling the gap. Bach turned the process on its head: he wrote a Mass with soloists, choir and orchestra and divided it into 'numbers' in Passion style. This was the *Mass in B minor*, and it set the pattern for countless masses by other composers; it ranks with the *St Matthew Passion* as one of the noblest religious works ever written.

EXPLORING BACH   Among Bach's shorter works we recommend 'Sheep May Safely Graze' (two flutes and strings), 'Jesu, Joy of Man's Desiring' (piano solo version) and the sprightly first movement of Brandenburg Concerto No. 4. From his longer works, we recommend Brandenburg Concerto No. 3, the church cantata *Wachet auf* ('Sleepers, Wake'), and the splendidly twangy, solo harpsichord *Italian Concerto*.

Now TRY   Bach: *Magnificat* (shorter and brisker); motet, *Singet dem Herrn* (the Psalm 'Sing to the Lord a new song', set in Passion style. Schütz, *The Christmas Story*. Brahms, *A German Requiem*.

BALLET

Telling a dramatic story in music and movement alone, without words, is an art as old as the human race. Stone Age wall-paintings show dancers mimicking hunts or the activities of gods. King David of Israel, the Bible tells us, 'danced before the Lord', and both the Greek philosopher Socrates and the Roman emperor Nero were enthusiastic amateur ballet dancers. Dance-drama is a major art form in many cultures, notably those of India and the Far East.

In Europe, ballet as we know it began in the Middle Ages, when nobles enjoyed (and sometimes took part in) lavish entertainments involving instrumental music, dance and song. These often told a story, usually taken from myth – the love of Venus and Adonis, for example, or the exploits of Herakles. In sixteenth-century France, when this kind of entertainment was professionalized and became theatrical, the kind of 'story-ballets' we know today were born.

Western ballet nowadays is of two kinds. Story-ballets use dance and mime to tell a coherent narrative: these are plays in dance. Abstract ballets concentrate on the dancers' skills and the patterns they make: these are theatrical spectacles, closer to rock shows than to drama. ('Modern dance' is often abstract.) In most ballets, music is only one part of a total experience in which movement, design, lighting and costumes are equal partners. None the less, ballets use some of the most appealing of all classical music, and it is frequently detached from the dance and performed in concert or on record.

HÉROLD, *La fille mal gardée*

This is one of the funniest ballets in the repertoire. The Widow Simone (a character like a pantomime dame, usually played by a man in drag) plans to marry her daughter Lise to rich, stupid Alain; Lise wants to marry Colas, her lover. The story is farce, and its setting is a spectacular village festival where everyone shows off their dance skills – even the Widow gets to perform her clog-dance. The clog-dance, with its 'diddly-diddly-diddly-diddly dum-dum-dum' rhythm on wood-blocks, is the hit number, both in the complete ballet and the orchestral suite made from it. (Good follow-ups: Adam, *Giselle*. Sullivan, *Pineapple Poll*.)

CHOPIN, *Les sylphides*

In this abstract ballet, girls in tutus and boys in tights make geometric patterns to a set of Chopin's best-loved piano pieces, arranged for orchestra. In the theatre, the ballet depends on the atmosphere created by sets and lighting, and on the dancing; on record, Chopin's music carries all before it. (Good follow-ups: Weber, *Spectre de la rose*; Schumann, *Carnaval* (ballet version).)

TCHAIKOVSKY, *The Sleeping Beauty*

This sumptuous ballet is based on the fairy tale of the princess doomed by a wicked fairy to sleep for a hundred years, until she's wakened by a handsome prince. Its story allows lavish scenery and costumes (the court; the enchanted palace), fine character dancing (the parents;

the fairies), plenty of crowd work, and superb parts for the Prince and Princess. Two highlights are often performed separately: the Rose Adagio, a tour de force of dance in which Princess Aurora, on her birthday, dances with each of her suitors in turn, and the Aurora *pas de deux* which is the climax of the final wedding celebrations. There is a popular suite from the music (including the hypnotically swaying waltz), and Act 2 is often recorded separately. (Good follow-ups: Tchaikovsky, *Swan Lake; The Nutcracker*. Prokofiev, *Cinderella*.)

SAINT-SAËNS, *The Dying Swan*

This five-minute solo dance was made famous in the 1920s by Anna Pavlova, who used it in her touring ballet show. It is performed to 'The Swan', the limpid cello solo from Saint-Saëns' *Carnival of the Animals*. The dancer, in tutu and with swan-feather head-dress, flutters, droops, twirls and subsides in a sequence of movements as technically challenging to perform as they are uplifting to watch. (Good follow-ups: Tchaikovsky, *Bluebird pas de deux*. Prokofiev, *Romeo and Juliet pas de deux*.)

STRAVINSKY, *Petrushka*

During the St Petersburg Easter Fair, a Showman brings out three puppets: Petrushka, the Ballerina and the Moor. They dance. Later, when the humans have gone, we see that Petrushka is tormented by his possession of human emotions, his enthralment to the Showman and his love for the Ballerina. He fights the Moor for her and is killed. The crowd gasps, until the Showman points out that he is just a puppet after all. Stravinsky's puppet-music is splendid, but best of all is his surging, high-

leaping, accordion-squeezing, bear-dancing evocation
of the Easter Fair. (Good follow-ups: Stravinsky, *The
Firebird*; Khachaturian, *Gayane*.)

OTHER BALLETS See pages 37, 55, 70, 99, 145, 163, 194,
195, 205.

BARBER
Adagio for Strings

This grave, sonorous music, a cathedral in sound for string
orchestra, begins with a line of melody moving in step up
and down from a single note. It is like someone quietly
humming or keening. Gradually, instrument after instrument joins in. Some play supporting harmonies, others echo
the tune. The sound grows ever more intense, layer by layer,
implacably, unhurriedly, as if we were climbing a hill.
Suddenly we reach the summit: a blaze of sound, the tune
throbbing out full-throated. The climax dies away, and the
music gradually unwinds again, until only a thin whisper is
left, a single voice which dies away to silence.

Barber originally wrote the *Adagio* as the slow movement
of a string quartet, but the conductor Toscanini saw that its
full power would only be released by the sixty or so strings
of a large symphony orchestra, and persuaded him to
arrange it. It was instantly successful, partly because of its
cradle-to-grave, 'all-human-life-is-here' scenario, and partly
because of the way it builds to such intensity from its single,
simple theme. On the day President Kennedy was
murdered, it was played almost continuously on US TV, and
so its solemn, heart-rending sounds reached the ears of
millions around the world.

BARBER   Samuel Barber (1910–81), unusually for a major composer, was a fine baritone, and made professional recordings of some of his own pieces. The *Adagio*, and a few other works, brought him fame at a fairly early age (mid-twenties), and for half a century thereafter he was one of the US's most respected composers, writing big works (concertos; operas) and winning every prize in sight.

BARBER'S VIOLIN CONCERTO   Barber wrote one of the most haunting of all twentieth-century violin concertos: a wistful first movement, a heartfelt slow movement and a fiery finale. Of all his works, this is the best follow-up to *Adagio for Strings*, even though it's on a bigger scale and for a different instrumental combination. Try it one movement at a time – and prepare to be seduced.

NOW TRY   Barber, Overture to *The School for Scandal* (lighter and jollier, but just as tuneful). Delius, *The Walk to the Paradise Garden*; Chausson, *Poème* for violin and orchestra. Fauré, Prelude, *Pelléas and Mélisande*.

BARTÓK
Romanian Folk Dances

These are a concert-hall version of the teeth-flashing, high-leaping dances favoured by Eastern European folk groups. Bartók first arranged them for piano, but they soon became popular in other forms: violin and piano, accordion band, café group (including cimbalom – the Hungarian instrument which is like a keyboardless piano, played with handfuls of felt-tipped hammers like chopsticks), and symphony orchestra.

Six tiny dances, each less than a minute long, are played one after another without stopping, to make a whirl of contrasting sounds. The first dance is in march rhythm, the second a slinky clarinet tune, the third a high wail for violins over a bagpipe-drone bass, the fourth a wistful slow waltz, the fifth a polka and the sixth a whirling csárdás in gypsy style.

BARTÓK Béla Bartók (1881–1945) trained as a concert pianist, and was for years professor of piano at the Budapest Royal Academy of Music. He began composing when he was twenty-one, and collecting folk music when he was twenty-six. By the 1920s he had gathered an archive of tens of thousands of wax cylinders used to record the music (this is still the biggest folk music collection in Europe), and had also become one of the best-known composers of the age. He went on balancing three careers (pianist, composer, musicologist) until the Nazis occupied his beloved Hungary in 1940 and he was forced to escape to the USA.

COLLECTING FOLK MUSIC Bartók began this work in 1905, travelling all over Central Europe and the Balkans. He recorded the music in two ways: on paper and on the hand-cranked, wax-cylinder machines of the time. He travelled on horseback, on foot or by cart, hugging the equipment, he says, like a baby against the jolting. The recordings were often hampered by the suspicions or shyness of the people. One year, for example, he set out to record lullabies – and found that women were not allowed to sing to strangers, so that the recordings are of crow-voiced old men who, he says, 'never held or crooned to an infant in their lives'.

NOW TRY   Folk music pieces by Bartók: *Allegro barbaro* (piano solo); *Contrasts* (clarinet, violin and piano; written for Benny Goodman, and recorded by him, Bartók and Josef Szigeti – a classic disc); *Dance Suite* (orchestra). Enescu, Romanian Rhapsody No. 1. Kódaly, *Dances of Galánta*.

BARTÓK
Concerto for Orchestra

Concertos for solo instruments are common; in this piece Bartók set out to showcase an entire orchestra. He wrote for the Boston Symphony Orchestra, and spent hours listening to them, making notes not just about single players (such as a harpist or lead trumpeter), but also about the sound of the whole group. In this concerto for a hundred soloists there is no hiding place: each section – woodwind, brass, percussion, strings – has its chance to shine.

But the Concerto offers more than mere show. Bartók poured into it all his longing for the homeland he had been forced to leave. He filled it with the colours and rhythms of Hungarian folk dance, and with nostalgic outbursts as passionate as film music. The first movement begins with a mysterious introduction, as if the orchestra were heaving itself awake, and then explodes into energetic dance. The second movement, 'Play of the couples', gives the same little tune to pairs of wind instruments in turn – bassoons, oboes, clarinets, flutes, trumpets – and then does the same again, with a third instrument chattering underneath each time. The third movement is a lament, the fourth is a delicate but rudely interrupted intermezzo, and in the finale fresh-faced folk dance meets classical-music cleverness in a riotous blend of csárdás and jazzy, brassy fugue.

BARTÓK IN THE US   Bartók's escape from war-torn Europe brought him nothing but misery. A patriot, he raged that he was powerless to help his Nazi-occupied country. Work was hard to find, and he contracted leukaemia. It was not until 1943 that Sergey Koussevitsky, conductor of the Boston Symphony Orchestra, came to his rescue, commissioning the Concerto for Orchestra and organizing performances of his music.

UP SHOSTAKOVICH   In the Concerto's fourth movement, a blameless little intermezzo is suddenly interrupted by a march tune from one of Shostakovich's symphonies, and the horns and trombones fall about with mockery, braying and farting – after which the intermezzo resumes its placid course. Shostakovich, by all accounts, was furious, but Bartók never apologized, and the whole thirty seconds remain one of the briefest, and oddest, 'jokes' in music.

NOW TRY   Bartók, The *Miraculous Mandarin*. Kódaly, *Háry János* Suite. Holst, *The Planets*. Bernstein, *Fancy Free*.

BARTÓK
Piano Concerto No. 3

Bartók wrote this work for his wife. She specialized in playing Bach, and this delicate concerto is the kind of music Bach might have written if he'd known about Hungarian folk music and twentieth-century harmony.

There are three movements. The first contrasts a folk-song-like tune with stormy keyboard scales and runs: it reminded one critic of goldfish alternately basking and darting. The second movement begins and ends with patterns of slow notes on strings, huge webs of sound against which the piano plays a pleading, insistent tune. In between, Bartók inserts 'insect' music: orchestral rustlings and flutterings, with jabs and stabs of piano notes. The last movement first contrasts a brisk, Bachy fugue and a hymn-like melody, and then triumphantly plays them both at once.

INSECT MUSIC   Bartók was fascinated by insect sounds. He wrote 'insect' pieces (with titles like *From the Diary of a Fly*) and 'insect' movements in longer works. The sounds that chiefly inspired him were wing-flutterings, cicada-chirps and the tiny scrabblings of insects' feet on walls. (He must have been blessed not only with sharp hearing, but also with extraordinarily silent surroundings. How many people ever hear a fly's feet scrabble?)

BARTÓK'S MUSIC   Before Bartók, composers adapted folk music to suit their own styles; Bartók was one of the first to change his style to suit folk music, filling his works with the jagged rhythms and colourful harmonies of popular Middle European music. In the 1920s audiences found his compositions ear-piercingly barbaric. One critic compared him to a demented blacksmith; another said that sitting through his music was like having teeth filled. It was not until the 1940s that he became one of the best-loved of all twentieth-century classical composers.

EXPLORING BARTÓK   Bartók left few small works. The best way to explore his music is to ease oneself into the longer works, one movement at a time. Good start-points: Concerto for Orchestra (second and last movements); *Music for Strings, Percussion and Celesta* ('insect' second movement; last movement); Piano Concerto No. 3 (all). His major compositions include *The Miraculous Mandarin*,

Piano Concerto No. 2, String Quartet No. 6 and the exotic
nightmare-opera *Bluebeard's Castle.*

NOW TRY Bartók, *Dance Suite*; Viola Concerto. Ravel,
Piano Concerto in G. Shostakovich, Piano Concerto No. 2 ;
Falla, Harpsichord Concerto.

BEETHOVEN
'Moonlight' Sonata (Piano Sonata No. 14, Op. 27 No. 2)

In his twenties, Beethoven was famous for improvising at
piano concerts: making the music up as he went along.
(This was less random than it sounds: he probably worked
to a pre-existing plan, as jazz or rock musicians do today.)
Listeners wrote of the 'poetry and passion' of his playing,
the 'flow of changing moods', and, as the quote below
shows, the way he mocked his audiences afterwards.

The 'Moonlight' Sonata is like one of those improvisations, written down. It plays continuously for about twelve
minutes, and has three distinct movements. The first, and
best known, is a slow, march-like tune over a rippling
accompaniment. It reminded one listener of moonlight over
Lake Lucerne – hence the sonata's nickname – but it also
gives an impression of 'frozen' emotion, as if grief had
become stone before our eyes. The second movement is a
graceful dance, briefly interrupted by storms before
resuming its placid way. The last movement is a torrent of
notes, the pianist storming up and down the keyboard – as
one writer put it – 'like a wild-eyed poet-madman of his art'.

BEETHOVEN   Ludwig van Beethoven (1770–1827) first
won fame as a performer. His piano playing, compositions
and unorthodox manners were the rage of musical Vienna

in the 1790s. But deafness cut short his performing career, and by his mid-thirties he was unable to hear any sounds at all. He began exploring inner worlds of feeling and emotion in his music. His later works have a sense of uncompromising grandness, of struggle leading to serenity, which leads some listeners to treat him as one of the noblest of all creative artists, on a par with such giants as Shakespeare and Leonardo da Vinci.

BEETHOVEN AT THE PIANO   The piano virtuoso Carl Czerny often saw Beethoven improvising. He wrote: 'He knew exactly how to work on his hearers. Often, his playing was so expressive, his ideas were so beautiful and original and his performance was so lively that not an eye was dry, the room was full of sobs. When this happened, Beethoven fell about laughing. "Fools!" he shouted at his tear-stained audience. "Who can live among such spoiled children?"'

NOW TRY   Beethoven, 'Pathétique' Sonata (Piano Sonata No. 8, Op. 13); 'Appassionata' Sonata (Piano Sonata No. 23, Op. 57). Chopin, Scherzo No. 2.

BEETHOVEN
Symphony No. 6, 'Pastoral'

Beethoven was quick-tempered, and the frustrations of deafness did nothing to ease his inner turbulence. He did, however, find peace of soul in the countryside, particularly the Vienna Woods and Austrian Alps. His music often captures a mood of ecstatic calm, a radiance which the Germans call *Innigkeit*, 'innerness', and the Pastoral Symphony links this quality with the countryside. It is no sound-picture of country scenes, giving us cowbells, lowing

sheep or hunting horns, but (as Beethoven said) 'recollec-
tions of country life', in which 'listeners are left to discover
the situations for themselves'. The music is mainly about
emotion, not events.

There are five movements, and Beethoven gave each a
title. The first, 'Awakening of happy feelings on arrival in
the country', is used every time TV advertisers want to
conjure up quiet fields, grazing cows, misty woods and hills,
and explores the mood in an unhurried way, as inevitably as
blossom opening on a branch. The second movement, 'Scene
by the brook', is a tranquil tune with an eddying, rippling
accompaniment. (This movement, most of all, is where
'ecstatic calm' resides.) The movement ends with bird-calls.

The third movement, 'Happy rustic gathering', a
cheerful, lumpish dance, is interrupted by the fourth
movement, a storm which begins with pattering raindrops
and grows to spectacular thunder (cellos and double-basses)
and lightning (violins forking high above the orchestra,
drums battering away below). The storm ebbs and leads to
the fifth movement, 'Shepherds' thanksgiving'. This recap-
tures the serenity and happiness of the symphony's opening,
and adds another element vital in Beethoven's music: the
expression of intense religious faith. This emotional
rounding off and deepening is what makes this a symphony
rather than, say, a 'rustic suite'. It is intellectually as well as
emotionally complete.

BEETHOVEN AND THE ORCHESTRA   Until Beethoven's
time, orchestras were dominated by strings. Wind and brass
provided colour and contrast rather than being part of the
music's core. Beethoven, however, treated all sections of the
orchestra as equal. He added more instruments to the wind
and brass, and beefed up the music given to such 'Cinderella'

instruments as bassoons, trumpets, violas and double-basses. Thus began the Romantic, 'big-orchestra' sound, which was to be developed by later composers.

NOW TRY   Beethoven, Symphony No. 7. Smetana, *Vltava*. Haydn, Symphony No. 102.

BEETHOVEN
Overture to *Egmont*

Goethe's *Egmont* is a Shakespeare-inspired history play about a sixteenth-century nobleman who led a rebellion against Philip II of Spain, was betrayed and beheaded. Beethoven wrote incidental music, including this overture, for a production of the play in 1810.

The overture sets the tragic mood in eight minutes of powerful music. The opening contrasts loud, slow chords with dragging wisps of melody; the feeling is of desolation, nobility, doom. The central section, longer and quicker, suggests battles and arguments, and is intermingled with tender love music (used in the play for Egmont's love for a beautiful peasant girl, the passion his enemies exploit to trap him). Finally, like the sun breaking through storm clouds, the overture ends with a brisk, bright march, complete with trumpet fanfares and gleeful piccolo shrieks.

BEETHOVEN'S DEAFNESS   The cause of Beethoven's deafness is a mystery. His father was a drunk, and tried to batter the boy into submission to make him a child prodigy, a second Mozart. Some doctors think that repeated blows to the head were what damaged Beethoven's hearing. Others blame a fall, or syphilis (probably inherited). Beethoven first complained of pain and buzzing in the ears when he was in his mid-twenties, and in 1802, when he was thirty-two, his deafness was diagnosed as progressive and incurable, inducing in him a near-suicidal depression that lasted for several months.

In later life Beethoven could hear nothing at all. People had to write down what they wanted to say to him, and turn him towards audiences to see applause. After his death a huge collection of ear-trumpets and patent remedies was discovered, and he is said to have tried even hypnotism and black magic in the desperate search for a cure.

Non-musicians are often amazed that someone who was totally deaf could go on composing. But composers need no actual sounds: they 'hear' music as they read or write the notes. Beethoven's tragedy was not creative sterility, but the personal isolation that his deafness caused – coupled, perhaps, with the fact that he could never hear his music aurally, sensuously, never share the pleasure of every other music-lover.

Now TRY   Beethoven, Overture to *Coriolan*; Symphony No. 5. Berlioz, Overture to *King Lear*. Brahms, *Tragic Overture*.

BEETHOVEN
Piano Concerto No. 4

Beethoven first played this concerto himself in 1808. It was the biggest concerto ever composed – but hardly the flashiest. Many concertos exploit the fact that the piano is a percussion instrument (whose sound is made by hammers hitting strings), by being full of virtuoso banging. But this concerto goes for serenity and smoothness, qualities more usually linked with strings or voices, and not at all easy to bring off on the keyboard. Angry outbursts are given to the orchestra, and the piano soothes rather than seethes.

The concerto has three movements. The first is like a placid conversation, with ideas passed between soloist and orchestra. Urgency comes only towards the end, with the cadenza (a solo showpiece, nagging away at the notes of the main theme), and a demented dash up and down the keyboard, as if to say 'So there!'. The slow movement contrasts gruff statements by the strings with gentle piano replies. Liszt was reminded of the story of Orpheus, singing in the Underworld to soothe the Furies. The third movement is a gigantic polka with calmer interludes.

'Placid conversation', 'gentle replies', 'polka' – none of these are usual in concertos. Beethoven's triumph is that while the work is playing, everything seems so natural that you never once think what an unusual piece it is.

BEETHOVEN'S PERSONALITY Beethoven was untidy and badly co-ordinated, and his deafness made him testy. In 1809 he became guardian of his nephew Karl, and his life was thereafter complicated by having an adolescent in the house. He planned his compositions on long, solitary walks in the woods, striding along waving his arms, beating time, shouting and humming – something which impressed everyone who thought that this was exactly how Romantic geniuses should do their work.

EXPLORING BEETHOVEN From Beethoven's shorter works, we recommend the piano solo *Für Elise*; the gorgeous song 'Adelaide'; Romance No. 2 (for violin and orchestra); and the Overture to *Fidelio*. From his longer works, we recommend the jolly Septet; the turbulent Piano Sonata No. 21, 'Waldstein'; the 'Rasumovsky' String Quartet

Op. 59 No. 3; the Violin Concerto and – his most famous composition – Symphony No. 5.

Now try Beethoven, Piano Concerto No. 3. Chopin, *Andante spianato and grand polonaise* (piano and orchestra version). Schumann, Piano Concerto.

BEETHOVEN
'Spring' Sonata (Sonata No. 5 for violin and piano)

Beethoven wrote this sunny piece in 1801. It is an outpouring of melody, an expression of happiness and serenity rivalling the Pastoral Symphony. The violin and piano are like two equal partners in a conversation, suggesting ideas, picking them up, developing them and passing them back.

The Sonata has four short movements. The first bubbles and soars, its clean sounds seeming to sweep the cobwebs of winter away for ever. The second is one of Beethoven's favourite 'river' pieces, a slow tune over murmuring accompaniment. The third is called Scherzo – 'joke' – and the joke is that the piano begins alone with a tune, and then the violin comes in a beat behind, as if the players are out of time. The last movement picks up the unflurried mood of the first movement. There are moments of storm and bluster along the way, but the cheerful first tune keeps coming back to restore the happy mood.

BEETHOVEN'S MUSIC Beethoven was the first major 'Romantic' composer. His early works (including this sonata) use standard eighteenth-century forms and style, but have an emotional boldness and openness that must have seemed daring to contemporary listeners. From his thirties onwards, he concentrated his music's inner power, personalizing it in a way few composers had done before.

Before Beethoven, even the most emotionally extrovert music was restrained, formal, decorous. After him, music seemed to express the composer's struggle with feelings and ideas, so that the sense of striving, that the finished work represented a triumph of will, became a major part of its effect. Whereas Haydn wrote more than a hundred and four symphonies and Mozart wrote forty-one, Beethoven produced no more than nine – and each of those was a titanic struggle. He was not the first ever 'genius' among composers, but he was the first to make the self-awareness of genius a main ingredient in each finished product. Neither music nor composers have ever been the same again.

Now TRY   Beethoven wrote nine other sonatas for violin and piano: good ones to sample are the Violin Sonata Op. 12 No. 2 and (the more serious) No. 9, the 'Kreutzer' Sonata. Try also his Piano Trio Op. 97, 'Archduke'. Music in similar mood by others: Mozart, Sonata No. 26 for violin and piano, K378. Schubert, Sonatina No. 1 for violin and piano.

BERG
Violin Concerto 'To the memory of an angel'

Manon, beloved daughter of Berg's friends Alma and Walter Gropius, contracted polio just after her eighteenth birthday, and died. Heartbroken, Berg wrote this concerto, to be, as he said, her 'Requiem'.

Berg's music was always written with a 'programme'. Here, the violin embodies Manon, and the orchestra

symbolizes the forces of life, then death, and finally angels
welcoming her into heaven.

The first movement, a musical portrait of Manon, begins
dreamily and tenderly, the solo violin soaring and yearning
above the orchestra. A folk song and a gentle waltz suggest
innocence, delicacy and vulnerability. The second movement begins with sombre lurches and heaves in the
orchestra (the ugliness of death), set against terrified sobs
and flutterings on the violin. After a huge discord (the
moment of death), the violin plays the hymn 'It is enough',
about acceptance, and the orchestra takes it up, the music
becoming ever more serene as Manon's soul is carried to
paradise.

BERG AND HIS MUSIC   Alban Berg (1885–1935) spent
his summers composing and walking in the Alps, and his
winters in the heady, quarrelsome goldfish bowl of 1920s–
30s Viennese artistic life. Six weeks after finishing the
Violin Concerto, he was bitten by a mosquito, and died soon
afterwards of malaria.

Berg's music contains enough 'secret' meanings (mathematical patterns; tunes based on musical letters in his
friends' names) to keep a universityful of professors busy for
decades. But it is also as romantic as film music. He was
haunted by the ugliness of death, an idea that appears in
work after work. His pieces can sound harsh and discordant
at first, but their emotional power grows more and more
engulfing with each hearing.

VIENNESE INTELLECTUALS   The Gropius family belonged to a group that led Viennese intellectual life for
decades, and Walter Gropius himself was head of the
Bauhaus (an avant-garde design institute). The philosopher
Max Weber, the painter Kokoschka, the poet Altenberg and

the composer Schoenberg were all members of the circle. At
its heart was Alma Gropius, whose first husband had been
the composer Gustav Mahler and who made herself the
patron (and sometimes the lover) of every promising young
genius in town.

NOW TRY   Berg, Chamber Concerto (first movement).
Bartók, Violin Concerto No. 1. Mahler, *Adagietto* (from
Symphony No. 5).

BERLIOZ
Roman Carnival Overture

Berlioz was never one to waste good ideas. He hoarded
scrag-ends and scraps of melody, waiting for the right work
to show them to best advantage – and if an idea was one of
his particular favourites, he used it several times.

Roman Carnival began in 1837, when Berlioz wrote an
opera about the medieval goldsmith-philosopher-adven-
turer Benvenuto Cellini. The opera wasn't a success, but it
had its quota of good tunes – and Berlioz pillaged them to
make this concert overture, first performed in 1843. Then,
repaying the loan, he stuck the overture into the opera as an
interlude, 'lifting' the atmosphere at one of the drama's
slacker moments.

After a preliminary swagger, as if the orchestra were
doing one of those swashbuckling bows where you stick out
one leg and sweep the floor with the feather in your cap, we
move straight to the main love theme. This appears first as a
solo on cor anglais (one of Berlioz's favourite instruments),
and then in canon on the strings, the cellos playing it a bar
or so behind the violins, as if we were eavesdropping on two
lovers' sweet nothings. Passion grows, until all the strings

are in a lather of ardour. Then, with another flourish, the carnival begins. The strings play a fast dance, accompanied by castanets, cymbals and frolicking woodwind. The lovers are briefly heard (love tune on solo horn), then gaiety takes us to the final, exhausted-but-happy chords.

BERLIOZ   Hector Berlioz (1803–69) was persuaded by his parents to study medicine, but he rebelled on his first day in the dissecting room and studied music instead. He outraged his professors by disagreeing with them, and they took their revenge in his adult life by blocking his progress as an officially approved writer of operas and choral works. He was obliged to organize his own performances, and began to mount gargantuan concerts, using orchestras of hundreds and choirs of thousands. Dazzle became his music's calling-card, and he mixed it with a kind of self-communing, romantic melancholy which makes his work unique.

NOW TRY   Berlioz, *Le Corsair* Overture. Dvořák, *Carnival* Overture. Nicolai, Overture to *The Merry Wives of Windsor*. Nielsen, Overture to *Maskarade*.

BERLIOZ
Symphonie fantastique

Symphonie fantastique is actually the subtitle of this piece. Berlioz's main title (now seldom used) was 'Episode in the Life of an Artist', and he wrote a note explaining how each of the five movements related to the main story.

Berlioz wrote the symphony in 1830, while he was in the throes of passion for Harriet Smithson, an actress he hadn't even met. In the symphony, he imagines a romantic young genius, thwarted in love, who takes opium and falls into a stupor during which he has fantastic dreams. The five movements are these dreams, and they are linked by an *idée fixe* ('fixed idea'), a tune which figures in each and represents the beloved.

The five movements are: 'Reveries, passions' (pictures of the artist's melancholy before he meets his beloved, his joy when he does so, and his despair when he loses her); 'A ball' (artist and beloved at an elegant, swirling waltz); 'In the country' (shepherds' pipes, rustling leaves, a thunderstorm – and 'she' is missing); 'March to the scaffold' (the artist's execution following his murder of his beloved); 'Witches' Sabbath' (the living dead – including, transformed, his beloved – dance and mock him, the *idée fixe* becoming a shriek of clarinets and a jeering fugue).

We can follow Berlioz's 'programme' in detail, almost bar by bar, and the musical strength of the work is shown by the fact that we can throw it away and simply enjoy Berlioz's glorious themes and stunning orchestral sound.

BERLIOZ AND THE ORCHESTRA Berlioz's constant search for novelty led him to experiment with orchestration, using unusual instruments wherever possible, and he set standards that have seldom been bettered since. He loved brass and percussion, and expected his first violinists to play with Paganini-like brilliance and energy. He once scoured a town he was visiting for a cor anglais player (then rare), interviewed two dozen people with instruments of all kinds except cor anglais, then finally found his player, only to have to start searching again when the man confessed he didn't own an instrument.

NOW TRY Berlioz, 'Queen Mab' Scherzo (from *Romeo and Juliette*); *Harold in Italy*; Overture to *King Lear*. Richard Strauss, *Till Eulenspiegel*; Elgar, 'Enigma' Variations.

BERNSTEIN
Overture to *Candide*

How to write the overture for a theatre show: Go through your score, picking plums – jazz riff, love song, show-stopper. Join them together and arrange for theatre band. Hundreds of overtures are made this way. Some composers (Rossini; Sullivan; even Mozart) waited until the last moment, handing them over with the ink still wet. Others left (and leave) them to arranger or conductor: pieceworkers with skill instead of inspiration.

Bernstein adopted this recipe for *Candide* and added genius. Instead of simply ramming the tunes together, he recrafted them, played games with them. One comes in canon, so that you hear it twice, slightly separated as if it's shadowing itself. The love song and show-stopper start quietly, then build and build until the whole orchestra is swooping, fizzing and crackling, high on energy and emotion. The scoring is not for Reliant Robin theatre band, but for Rolls-Royce full orchestra. All this in four minutes, so that (in true showbiz style) it slays you in the aisles, leaves you panting for more. Even Bernstein, that musical magician, seldom worked a trick to equal this one.

CANDIDE Candide blends opera and Broadway show. The story is satire, about an innocent who never doubts the honesty and morality of the world, despite being conned and cheated at every step. The book is sharp and the lyrics are as witty as Cole Porter's. The music veers from spoof Mozart to big-band jazz tunes. Because the show is neither opera nor musical, it took some time to make its name, but succeeded in the 1980s, thanks partly to a starry CD set which was one of Bernstein's last recordings. But the overture has had no such problems: for over thirty years, it's been one of classical music's favourite lollipops.

BERNSTEIN　Leonard Bernstein (1918–90) could have made separate careers as conductor, composer, pianist, professor, TV personality, writer – and instead he combined them all. He wrote Broadway shows, film music, symphonies, church works and jazz ballets. He was a superstar, and his passionate, often-stated belief that music challenges and satisfies our minds and emotions more than any other art lives on in every note he wrote.

NOW TRY　Bernstein, the rest of *Candide*; Symphonic Dances from *West Side Story*. Nielsen, Overture to *Maskarade*. Chabrier, *Joyeuse marche*.

BERNSTEIN
West Side Story

Bernstein's best-loved work exists in many forms. It began as a stage musical and is often revived. It was filmed in 1961 with some of the most dazzling dancing ever put on film, and has since been recorded several times, from the original-cast discs of the 1960s to the 1980s set conducted by Bernstein and featuring such stars as Kiri Te Kanawa and José Carreras – a feast of singing. In the 1970s Bernstein extracted the best numbers and arranged them for orchestra alone (the Symphonic Dances). Listening to this, you miss the voices but can revel in something not always uppermost in the theatre or on film: Bernstein's scintillating orchestral writing.

Different stage musicals offer different pleasures. *Kiss Me, Kate* has unbeatable lyrics; *Guys and Dolls* has a fascinating story; *Cats* is a dazzle of dance. *West Side Story* has them all: the book by Arthur Laurents (with a little help from Shakespeare), lyrics by Stephen Sondheim, choreography by Jerome Robbins, music by Bernstein. For many it is the ultimate in musicals.

WEST SIDE STORY The story updates Shakespeare's *Romeo and Juliet*, setting it among teenage gangs in the ghettos of New York. The Jets and Sharks war to the death – for honour, for nothing – and when Maria (Jet) and Tony (Shark) fall in love, the outcome can only be tragedy. Bernstein's and Robbins's brilliant idea turned the gangs into rival groups of dancers, and contrasted their jazzy fights and songs ('The Rumble'; 'Gee, Officer Krupke') with the doomed, lyrical ecstasy of the love music ('Maria').

BERNSTEIN'S MUSIC Bernstein's other Broadway shows include *On the Town* (filmed with Frank Sinatra and Gene Kelly) and *Candide*. He also wrote ballets (*Fancy Free*), film music (*On the Waterfront*) and a showpiece for Benny Goodman (*Prelude, Fugue and Riffs* – a million times more fun than its title), and three heavyweight symphonies, a Mass and the *Chichester Psalms*, which spice the style of English cathedral music with wicked, jazzy rhythms.

NOW TRY Bernstein, *On the Town* (film; musical; ballet; Symphonic Dances). Frank Loesser, *Guys and Dolls* (musical; film); *Seven Brides for Seven Brothers* (film musical, with dancing to rival any in *West Side Story*).

BIZET
Suites from *L'Arlésienne*

Nineteenth-century theatre-goers liked lavish incidental music, and to provide this most theatres had pit bands, ranging from two or three players to full orchestras. Writing music for plays financed many composers' lives. L'Arlésienne ('The Girl from Arles') was a tragedy by the Provençal writer Alphonse Daudet, first performed in Paris in 1872. Bizet was asked to write the incidental music: a dozen numbers, ranging from a few mood-setting bars to preludes and interludes lasting several minutes. He had an orchestra of twenty-six, and the management requested 'Provençal musical styles' to match Daudet's Southern dialect.

Daudet's play is long forgotten, but Bizet subsequently worked the best numbers from his music into two orchestral suites, and these are now among his most popular, most tuneful works. The movements range from folk dances (the swaggering Prelude to Suite No. 1, the famous Farandole from Suite No. 2) to sound-pictures of the countryside, love scenes and church bells ringing out on Sunday morning. Suite No. 1 (Prelude, Minuet, Adagietto, Carillon) is better known than Suite No. 2, but conductors often cheat and add the best movements of Suite No. 2 (especially the final Farandole).

BIZET Georges Bizet (1838–75) was a musical prodigy, beginning his career as concert pianist and prize-winning composer at the age of eleven. His ambition was to succeed in the theatre, and all his life, while supporting himself by hack work (arranging other people's music for publishers, copying scores), he planned, wrote and rewrote operas of every kind, from a tragedy about Ivan the Terrible to frothy farce. Only a few projects actually reached the stage, and all were flops. The last and biggest disaster was *Carmen* in 1875 – and Bizet died soon afterwards.

BIZET'S MUSIC   Bizet admired Rossini, and imitated his perky scoring and penchant for a good tune. He envied the heavyweights of tragic opera, and tried to write sombre, emotion-racked music in grandest style. He succeeded with the lighter side, and (except in *Carmen*) failed with tragedy. He said bitterly that he was 'too facile', but the world has ever since been grateful for his unfailing zest and flair: the light thing done to perfection, every time.

NOW TRY   Bizet, Overture to *Doctor Miracle*; Symphony in C. Grieg, *Peer Gynt* Suite No. 1. Edward German, *Henry VIII* Suite.

BIZET
Carmen

When Tchaikovsky saw *Carmen* in 1875 he prophesied that it would be the best-known opera in the world. At the time he was the only person who thought so; the rest of the first-night audience was shocked and outraged. The plot glamorized smugglers, gypsies and criminals, they said. It showed a woman dancing half-naked – and, worse, smoking cigarettes. It was about passionate, unmarried love (two men rivals for one woman), and culminated in a bloody knife-murder, centre-stage. Audiences of the time loved 'exotic' stories in their operas, and 'realism', but this was going too far.

What Tchaikovsky noticed (and seemingly no one else) was how glorious Bizet's music was. *Carmen* may have a sordid story, acted out in wooden dialogue (especially lumpish, the way some opera singers perform it), but its music is colourful, heart-on-sleeve emotional, superbly dramatic and crammed with tunes. Soon after the production flopped, the gypsy choruses, the swaggering Toreador's Song and Carmen's sultry, seductive 'Habanera' were extracted, performed separately, sold as sheet music and as rolls for barrel-organs (the ancestors of gramophones). Their popularity was worldwide, and brought the opera back to the stage, where it has been a blockbuster ever since.

LISTENING TO *CARMEN*   As with all operas, the best way to enjoy *Carmen* is to see it on-stage, or in one of the many productions on video. The Toreador's Song, the Flower Song and 'Habanera' are hits on their own, unfailingly popular both as songs and as instrumentals. (They make a good start-point for anyone new to *Carmen*.) Bizet organized extracts from the music into a *Carmen* Prelude and a *Carmen* Suite, both of which catch all the opera's passion and colour, and give you all the tunes, in pocket form.

NOW TRY   Individual numbers: Bizet, 'Au fond du temple saint' (from *The Pearl Fishers*); Serenade from *The Fair Maid of Perth*. Leoncavallo, 'On With the Motley' (from *I Pagliacci*). Verdi, 'Caro nome' (from *Rigoletto*). Preludes and suites: Bizet, *Jeux d'enfants* (orchestral suite); Chabrier, *España*; Falla, 'Ritual Fire Dance' (from *Love the Magician*); Smetana, Overture (or complete suite) from *The Bartered Bride*. Complete opera: Verdi, *Il Trovatore*.

BORODIN
Polovtsian Dances from *Prince Igor*

The Polovtsians were a Central Asian people who fought the Russians in the twelfth century. In 1890 Borodin wrote an opera, *Prince Igor*, about this war – or rather about the tragic love of a Polovtsian princess for a Russian prince. In Act 2 the Polovtsians take the captured prince to their desert camp, treat him with honour, and hold a banquet with lavish entertainment of singing and dancing (wild by the men, seductive by the women), and a wealth of whirl and colour. To our ears, these tunes blend Far Eastern exoticism and gypsy lilt, and Borodin's scoring is a blur of castanets, tambourines, shrilling woodwind and surging strings.

Borodin's heady music was too good to leave embedded in a rarely performed opera. It was soon extracted and became a bring-the-house-down concert-hall piece, a ballet, and the source of the stage musical *Kismet*. ('Hold my hand, I'm a stranger in Paradise' was that show's hit song, and it is the main tune of the Dances.)

BORODIN   Alexander Borodin (1833–87) was a Sunday composer, working during the week as a doctor and university professor. He belonged to a group of composers who called themselves 'The Mighty Handful', and who tried, in their music, to revitalize the folk traditions and styles of ancient Russia. Borodin's chosen area was Central Asia, the one-time home of such conquerors as Genghis Khan and Tamerlane the Great. The music of this area fascinated Borodin: even when he wrote symphonies or string quartets, the folk rhythms, exotic harmonies and skirling tunes of the East keep bursting in.

FOLK DANCING   On-stage, the *Polovtsian Dances* are fast
and furious. To stop the dancers dropping from exhaustion,
no one person performs throughout. Small groups, or
individuals, take turns to whirl, leap and cartwheel for a
couple of minutes at a time, and then give way to others, so
that the show is continuous. When Stalin wanted to show
off the different parts of the Soviet Union, he formed dance
groups to perform regional folk dances – and borrowed
Borodin's idea. Consequently, the *Polovtsian Dances* tend
to remind us of such groups as the Red Army Ensemble,
even though the influence is actually entirely the other way
around.

NOW TRY   Borodin, *In the Steppes of Central Asia*;
Symphony No. 1. Rimsky-Korsakov, *Sheherazade*. Stravinsky, *The Firebird* Suite.

BOULEZ
Répons

All music consists of organized sounds, and uses the same
basic ingredients: pitch (the height or depth of each sound),
distance between sounds, length of sounds and silences. For
the last thousand years, these ingredients have been mixed
in much the same way everywhere. When we hear a new
piece, we can usually relate it to what has gone before.

Boulez takes each sound ingredient and uses it in an
entirely original way. *Répons* is a good introduction to his
sound-world, not only typical but accessible and splendid –
a masterpiece. If you are listening to a recording, it needs
good stereo to make its full effect: headphones are better
than speakers. Best of all, it should be heard live, in the
concert hall: a rare but rewarding treat.

Répons uses six soloists and a small orchestra. The audience sits in a circle, and the players sit among them and around them. The sounds are fed through a computer, whose operator modulates them, changing them electronically. Computer and players 'challenge' each other, by proposing sounds and responding (hence the piece's name). This is the way jazz or Indian music are made, applied to avant-garde sound. Mostly, the piece is hypnotic and discreet, tickling the ear; but every so often a flurry of virtuoso improvisation breaks out, a miniature sound-orgy.

BOULEZ   Pierre Boulez (born 1925) has two careers. He is a high-profile conductor, specializing in twentieth-century music, and a tireless experimental composer, using mathematical systems to 'program' his inspiration and computers and electronics to modulate live sound. From 1979 he headed IRCAM, a studio dedicated to experiments in acoustics and music, and it was for his co-workers at IRCAM that *Répons* was conceived.

RANDOMNESS   Boulez uses improvisation because it allows chance into music – and he also places trust in chance in other ways. An orchestra once rang to ask the title of a set of songs he was writing, so that they could print the programme. He said, 'All I can tell you is, e. e. cummings wrote the poems' – and was delighted when this was duly printed as the title.

NOW TRY   Boulez, *Éclat/Multiples*; *Notations*. John Cage, Sonatas and Interludes for prepared piano (one with objects stuck between the strings). Ligeti, *Lontano*.

BRAHMS
'How Lovely Are Thy Dwellings Fair'

This favourite movement from Brahms's *A German Requiem* is often heard on its own. It is a musical picture of souls on Earth being granted a glimpse of Paradise. Flute and clarinet begin, with a downward-stepping tune like a ray of light from heaven. At once the choir sings the same tune, but moving upwards, as if gazing into Paradise: 'How lovely are thy dwellings fair, O Lord of Hosts'. The music grows turbulent, as they sing 'My soul longeth, yea, fainteth, for the courts of the Lord', and then, as they picture angels singing, the calm opening tune appears again. There is a short, lumbering fugue on the words 'They praise thy name evermore', and the piece ends in the sunlit serenity with which it began.

A GERMAN REQUIEM: In nineteenth-century Europe, one of the ways to prove that you were a 'senior composer' was to write a large-scale work for chorus and orchestra, to a Christian religious text. Brahms was not a believer, and refused to write a specifically Christian piece. Instead, he chose his own words from the Bible: words of regret for death and comfort for the bereft. There are seven movements, including two barnstorming fugues and a radiant solo soprano aria. The *Requiem* made Brahms's name, and his fortune; from the time of its first performance in 1869, he was accepted as the 'senior composer' he'd aspired to be.

BRAHMS Johannes Brahms (1833–97) trained as a pianist as well as a composer. In his twenties he made a living by playing, conducting choirs and writing easygoing works that would have a wide, quick sale, but from the time of *A German Requiem*, he made his living entirely from composing. Many people considered him Germany's greatest composer since Beethoven, and he lived up to this reputation by producing some of the grandest symphonies, concertos, sonatas and other large-scale works written that century.

NOW TRY   Brahms, 'Ye Now Have Sorrow' from *A German Requiem*; *Liebesliederwalzer* (waltzes for choir and piano duet); *Alto Rhapsody* (sensuously tragic piece for alto, choir and orchestra). After 'How Lovely': Mozart, 'Ave verum corpus'. Verdi, *Stabat mater*. After the whole *German Requiem*: Elgar, *The Dream of Gerontius*.

BRAHMS
Academic Festival Overture

In 1879 the University of Breslau gave Brahms an honorary degree. They asked him to write something for the university orchestra – and hoped for a symphony. Instead, he wrote this Overture.

Since medieval times, German students had formed Music Guilds and Drinking Clubs (really the same thing), where they met – you've guessed – to sing and drink. Over the years, many of the songs had become traditional, and were part of every student's growing up. Brahms's overture treats these songs like serious musical themes. The result is a mixture of poker-faced symphonic music and medley – and even today, when the songs are otherwise forgotten, the work's colour and exuberance are irresistible, from the mock-serious opening to the solemn trumpet tune in the middle (a tune whose riotous words every student in the audience would have known), and the blaze of sound which ends the overture with the most famous student song of all, 'Gaudeamus igitur' ('Let's live it up while still we're young').

BRAHMS'S MUSIC   Brahms was an intellectual composer, interested in such grand musical structures as symphony and sonata. His works are magnificently crafted; he was a 'composer's composer', setting himself complex problems and solving them with dazzling ingenuity. But he was also a Romantic, a creator of heart-stopping tunes and melting harmonies. The mixture is heady: you can wallow in a Brahms piece for its sensuous sound alone, then listen again and again, discovering new beauty, and new subtlety, each time.

BRAHMS'S CHARACTER   Brahms, a reclusive bachelor, was famous for being one of the rudest men in Germany. (He once turned to the aghast guests as he left a dinner-party, and said, 'If there's anyone here I haven't offended, I apologize.') He was a trying friend, affectionate one day and offhand the next. But if you persevered he could be loyal, generous – and endlessly stimulating. He was married to his work, people said: his energy went into his music, and his gruffness was a small price to pay for the magnificence of every work he wrote. (Even so, there was another side to his character: see page 43.)

NOW TRY   Brahms, Variations on a Theme by Haydn. Wagner, Prelude to *The Mastersingers*. Elgar, *Cockaigne* Overture.

BRAHMS
Symphony No. 1

All Brahms's strengths are in this stunning piece. It has whistleable tunes, seductive orchestral sound and kaleidoscopic contrasts. It is one of the grandest symphonies since Beethoven's Ninth (it used to be nicknamed 'Beethoven's Tenth') – a cathedral of a piece, sounding as if created from granite and stained glass, not ink and paper. Brahms poured into it everything he'd learned in half a composing lifetime. It is a monument in the class of Shakespeare's tragedies or Michelangelo's statues – and, like them, however forbidding it may seem at first, it's perfectly accessible and grows more impressive the more you get to know it.

There are four movements. The first begins in grinding agony, as if the notes were being forced out of the orchestra under extreme pressure, and runs the gamut of emotion before collapsing in a kind of exhausted quiet. The second builds vast arches of sound on a simple, slow melody. The third provides contrast to all the striving: limpid, melodious, ungrand. The fourth begins slowly, builds to a climax and then introduces a tune which is second cousin to the big tune of Beethoven's Ninth Symphony. (Someone bravely asked Brahms if he'd noticed this. 'Any fool can see that,' he growled.) Instead of the striving of the first movement, this one is bluff and bracing: a route march for the mind.

THE LIGHTER BRAHMS   Brahms was not all gruffness, however. The children of Vienna saw a completely different side to him. Every morning he used to walk to his favourite coffee-house – and his pockets were always stuffed with sweets and coins. 'Anyone who can jump as high as this gets a prize,' he would say, holding out his arm. As the children leapt, his arm rose higher and higher, and by the time he arrived at the coffee-house he was like the Pied Piper, surrounded by a giggling, delighted throng.

EXPLORING BRAHMS   From Brahms's shorter pieces, we recommend the Hungarian Dances for orchestra, the songs 'Vain Serenade' and 'Lullaby', and the piano solo Waltzes Op. 39 and Four Piano Pieces Op. 119. From his longer works, we recommend the Variations on a Theme by Haydn for orchestra, the sombre Four Serious Songs and the lyrical Clarinet Quintet.

NOW TRY   Brahms, Symphony No. 2; Double Concerto. Beethoven, Symphony No. 7. Tchaikovsky, Symphony No. 5.

BRITTEN
Four Sea Interludes

These pieces from Britten's opera *Peter Grimes* are well known as a concert-hall item. Each is a sound-picture of one aspect of life in a small East Anglian fishing village. The first depicts the desolation of the open sea. High violins and flutes wail like seagulls. Waves heave and toss (brass), foam glitters in the sun (clarinets). The second movement, 'Sunday morning', is a jangle of bells as people set out for the village church. There is a chatter of gossip (woodwind), swelling to anger – they are muttering about the loner Peter Grimes – and then dying away as the people pass inside for the service. The third movement, 'Moonlight', begins quietly, sinisterly, with sliding string chords and spiky, glinting sounds from the flutes. In the opera, the interlude depicts Grimes's mental anguish, and rises to a huge cry of despair. In the suite, it leads without a break into the fourth movement, a pounding storm.

BRITTEN Benjamin Britten (1913–76) was a child prodigy, and was making his living as a professional composer by the age of eighteen. He specialized in vocal music (song-sets and operas), but also wrote dazzling instrumental works, including one of the best known of all orchestral show-pieces, known officially as Variations and Fugue on a Theme of Purcell and unofficially as *The Young Person's Guide to the Orchestra* (after an educational film of the 1940s, for which it was the score). With Peter Pears, he founded the Aldeburgh Festival, still second only to Edinburgh in British musical life.

SERENADE Britten wrote many works for Pears's beautiful voice. The Serenade is scored for solo tenor, horn and string orchestra. It sets seven poems about night, ranging from the tortured 'O rose, thou art sick' (shrieks of agony from the horn) to the dancing 'Queen and huntress', about Diana, goddess of the Moon, and the ravishing 'O soft embalmer of the still midnight', an invocation of sleep which closes the whole work. Unforgettable music, superbly recorded by Pears with Denis Brain in the 1960s and with Barry Tuckwell in the 1970s – each a classic.

NOW TRY Britten: *Sinfonia da requiem*; *Soirées musicales*. Bax, *Tintagel*. Tippett, *Ritual Dances*.

CHAMBER MUSIC

Chamber music, as its Italian name *musica da camera* suggests, should really be called 'room music'. The essential element is the small number of players it needs: no more than can fit in a fair-sized room. In practice, chamber music is written for groups of from two to about eleven players (at which point the ensemble becomes a 'chamber' orchestra).

Chamber works are usually named after the number of players taking part: trios, quartets, quintets, sextets, septets, octets and nonets. The exception is duos – these were originally called 'duo-sonatas' and are now generally just 'sonatas'.

EARLY CHAMBER MUSIC

In the sixteenth and seventeenth centuries, chamber works were often performed by amateurs. Paintings show three or four people sitting round a single music stand, playing recorders, viols or a mixed group of instruments such as flute, lute and bass. Composers wrote short pieces (fantasias) and arranged popular tunes for this market. We recommend the 'consorts' of Anthony Holborne at the chirpy end of the market, and, at the serious end, the fantasias for viols written by Ferrabosco and Purcell.

Later in the seventeenth century, Italian composers invented the 'sonata' (from *musica sonata*, 'played music': that is, for instruments not voices). Sonatas are abstract works, without stories, and come in several movements. Apart from opera, they are the longest-lasting of all classical-music forms, surviving almost unchanged from about 1650 to the present. In the 1700s a

sonata might have been written for one instrument
alone, or for one instrument with accompaniment
(usually continuo, that is, keyboard and bass viol).
Sonatas for two instruments and accompaniment were
called 'trio-sonatas' – confusingly so, since if the
accompaniment used continuo, four players were involved, not three. From this period we recommend the
sonatas of Corelli and the trio-sonatas of Telemann (no
specific works, as all are equally good).

LATER CHAMBER MUSIC

As chamber music developed, a gulf began to appear
between works for amateurs and for professionals.
Amateur works were usually written as teaching pieces
or for simple home enjoyment, and tended to be smaller-
scale and easier. (This didn't always affect the quality of
the music: Haydn's and Mozart's piano sonatas and
trios, for example, are some of their most delightful
works.) Chamber music for professional performers
tended either to be written for entertainment (good
examples are Mozart's serenades and divertimentos,
intended to be played at aristocratic banquets and
parties) or were large-scale works similar to symphonies
or concertos except that they used small groups of
players. (For the entertainment type, we recommend
Mozart's Serenade No. 11 for wind instruments, K375,
one of his own favourite works. For works on a larger
scale, we recommend Haydn's String Quartet Op. 76 No.
3.) Occasionally, composers combined both types of
music, writing entertainment works that could be
played by either amateurs or professionals, and which
made no compromises about difficulty or quality:

Beethoven's Septet and Schubert's Fantasy in F minor for piano duet are glorious examples.

CHAMBER MUSIC IN CONCERT

A somewhat unlikely development, from Beethoven's time onwards, was the appearance of 'chamber concerts', not in people's homes but in concert halls, before paying audiences. These demanded a new kind of chamber music – written for small groups, certainly, but otherwise on the largest and grandest scale. The duo-sonatas, trios, quartets and other works of nineteenth- and twentieth-century composers contain some of their most expansive thoughts, and even the humble solo sonata grew, in many composers' hands, into a major form, a sort of symphony for single player. This kind of chamber music was worlds away from the 'sonatinas' and 'miniature quartets' written for teaching or for amateurs, which rarely appeared in professional concerts. Often, it contained a composer's most intimate thoughts – a challenge to listeners, but one which offers rare rewards.

RECOMMENDATIONS

This is only a small sample of the riches available. All the works are accessible, and some are among the masterpieces of the genre.

Start here: Fauré, *Après un rève* (cello and piano). Arnold, *Three Shanties* (wind quintet). Milhaud, *Scaramouche* (two pianos). Beethoven, Septet.

Trios: Haydn, 'Gypsy Rondo' Trio. Ibert, *Trois Pièces Brèves.* Dvořák, 'Dumky' Trio.

Quartets: Mozart, 'Dissonance' String Quartet, K465. Beethoven, 'Rasumovsky' String Quartet Op. 59 No. 3.

Quintets: Schubert, 'Trout' Quintet. Brahms, Clarinet Quintet. Mozart, Quintet in G Minor, K516. Nielsen, Wind Quintet.

Larger groups: Mendelssohn, Octet. Stravinsky, Octet. Ravel, Introduction and Allegro. Gounod, *Petite Symphonie* for wind instruments. Mozart, 'Gran Partita' Serenade for Thirteen Wind Instruments, K361.

CHOPIN
Fantasy-Impromptu

This piano show piece asks the player to perform one of the hardest of all musical feats: playing two different rhythms simultaneously, one in each hand. While the right hand plays fast groups of four notes, the left hand plays groups of three – producing a sound effect like sparks from a Catherine wheel. There follows a slow tune (made into the never-to-be-forgotten popular song, 'I'm always chasing rainbows'), and then the fast music reappears, this time setting groups of five against three, to keep both pianist and audience alert.

CHOPIN'S MUSIC   Chopin wrote most of his music for piano, to play himself. He specialized in pieces with poetic titles (nocturnes, ballades, preludes), and in such dances as waltzes and mazurkas. By all accounts, his playing combined dazzling technique with a kind of dreamy melancholy – and these are the qualities he put into his compositions.

LES SYLPHIDES *Les sylphides* ('The Nymphs') is a ballet made from some of Chopin's most popular pieces. The music is, alas, arranged for orchestra, and loses the delicacy and fire of the piano originals. None the less, it makes a beautiful, autumnal ballet, and it's a handy introduction to Chopin for anyone who can bear the absence of the piano.

WHAT TO LISTEN TO Chopin is a superb composer for 'anthology' concerts or recordings: a nocturne, some studies, a waltz, perhaps a ballade, setting each other off like flowers in a garden. You can also buy the works in groups of the same kind: 4 scherzos, 10 polonaises, 25 preludes, and so on. The most satisfying (as sets) are the Nocturnes, headily poetic, and the firework-show Studies. Some pieces have nicknames, but these mean little. The 'Minute Waltz', for example, lasts longer than a minute; the 'Raindrop' Prelude, though a patter of brisk, short notes, is less reminiscent of rain than the more boringly nicknamed 'Black Key Study'.

NOW TRY Chopin, Berceuse; *Grande valse brillante* Op. 18; Nocturne, Op. 32 No. 2. Liszt, 'La Campanella' (from *Transcendental Studies*); Debussy, 'Clair de lune' (from *Suite bergamasque*; Godowsky, *Paraphrases on Chopin's Studies* (pieces running two, sometimes three, of Chopin's already formidable studies together, until you wonder how many hands the player has).

CHOPIN
Piano Concertos Nos. 1 and 2

Chopin wrote two show-piece concertos in his late teens, while he was still making a career as a virtuoso pianist. He had only a sketchy notion of how to write for orchestra, with the result that some of the orchestral players sit and mope, with no more than a few dozen notes to play in a whole half hour. But the solo piano part makes up for this. The first movements are beefy and showy, the second movements dreamily romantic, and the finales are skitters of notes based on tunes which stick in the mind like burrs.

CHOPIN Fryderyk Chopin (1810–49) first played in public at the age of eight. He was a professional virtuoso until he was twenty-one, then gave up this career for teaching and composing. He lived mainly in France, and had a stormy affair with the novelist George Sand. (She wrote a fascinating book about a winter they spent together on Majorca: sunny at first, then nothing but pouring rain, rows and sulks.) Chopin retired from public life because of frail health (he suffered from TB); but he never lost his love of being lionized by beautiful women at parties, and was always happy to sit down and play, pretending each time that being asked came as a delightful surprise.

SCHUMANN ON CHOPIN Schumann once described Chopin playing two of his own Studies (Op. 25, Nos. 1 and 2), and although the account is well over the top, it does give an idea of the extraordinary effect Chopin must have had on his listeners. If a hard-headed professional responded like this, what must ordinary fans have felt? 'Imagine that an Aeolian harp could play every note available, and that a genius's hand blended them in every kind of exotic decoration, but so that you could still hear profound underlying harmony and a softly singing melody. This is what the first study was like – and when it ended you felt as you do after a vision, a dream of happiness, which you force yourself back to sleep to dream again. He then played the second piece: delicate, soft, delightful, like a child singing in its sleep ...'

Now TRY Chopin, *Andante spianato and grand polonaise* (piano-and-orchestra version); Scherzo No. 2 (solo piano). Litolff, Scherzo from *Concerto symphonique* No. 4. Schumann, Piano Concerto.

CONCERTOS

EARLY CONCERTOS

In madrigals and other vocal works from the Renaissance, composers wrote 'concerto' over sections they wanted to be performed simply by instruments, without voices. From this, the word came to mean orchestral music of any kind. At first, concertos used no soloists. But early orchestras were often conducted by the lead violinist, and the custom arose of giving him or her a small amount of showy solo music. Inevitably, this amount grew bigger and bigger, until by the end of the seventeenth century 'concerto' came to have the meaning it has today: a piece for orchestra with one or more soloists.

As its name suggests, the concerto was invented in Italy, and was a speciality of Italian orchestras and soloists until about 1700, when it spread all over Europe. Violin concertos were the most popular, perhaps because of the lead-violin origins of the form. The earliest Italian concerto composer whose works are still played, Arcangelo Corelli (1653–1713), was the Paganini of his day, credited with almost magic skills; another composer of the time, Vivaldi, was as famous for his fiery playing as for the beauty of his music.

As well as concertos for single soloist and orchestra,

composers at the turn of the eighteenth century also composed *concerti grossi* ('large concertos'). These used a group of soloists, sometimes even a small band, set against the main orchestra. *Concerti grossi* were often 'large' in another way: instead of the three movements (fast–slow–fast) of the traditional solo concerto, they might have four, five or even six movements.

Good examples of solo concertos from this time are Vivaldi's Oboe Concerto No. 1 and Bach's Violin Concerto No. 2. For concerti grossi, we recommend Corelli's Christmas Concerto (Concerto Grosso in G minor, Op. 6 No. 8) and Handel's Concerto Grosso Op. 3 No. 1. All these composers wrote many other concertos in similar styles, so that there are plenty of follow-ups (over 400 in Vivaldi's case alone).

EIGHTEENTH-CENTURY CONCERTOS
For most of the eighteenth century symphonies were the main kind of orchestral music. Concertos were rarer and were thought of as more special. Often (as with Haydn's Trumpet Concerto), they were written for artists the composer particularly admired, or (as with Mozart's Concerto for Flute and Harp), for patrons who commissioned works for the instruments they themselves played. A few composers still wrote concertos for their own use. The best example is Mozart, whose forty-seven concertos include five for violin (written when he was nineteen, working for the Archbishop of Salzburg), and twenty-seven for piano (written to play at his own public concerts).

VIRTUOSO CONCERTOS
The arrival of the nineteenth century brought a change. Virtuoso performers such as Nicolò Paganini began to

make their mark, dazzling audiences with the fireworks of their technique. Instruments, too, were made larger and more powerful. Wind instruments and brass instruments were equipped with keys and valves, which provided them with far more notes, and made them more easy to play. Pianos began to replace the smaller harpsichords and fortepianos, and the invention of the metal-frame piano made it possible vastly to increase the tension on the strings, allowing two or even three strings to each note and so enormously heightening the instrument's power.

One result of this increase in instrumental potential was a sudden demand for big, heroic concertos, almost like contests between soloist and orchestra. A few composers still wrote 'conversational' concertos, but from Beethoven's 'Emperor' Concerto (Piano Concerto No. 5) onwards, the main accent was on display. Nineteenth-century concertos are some of the biggest, most glittering works in the entire concert repertoire. Good samples are Bruch's Violin Concerto No. 1, Brahms's Violin Concerto and the first piano concertos of Liszt and Tchaikovsky.

LATER CONCERTOS

Many twentieth-century composers went on writing big, beefy concertos in nineteenth-century style. Of these, few works can beat the panache of Rachmaninov's Piano Concerto No. 2, Walton's Violin Concerto or Shostakovich's witty Piano Concerto No. 2. But people were also rediscovering the joys of eighteenth-century music, and many composers wrote concertos imitating its restrained, unflashy style. We recommend Françaix's delectable Piano Concertino, Rodrigo's *Fantasia para un gentilhombre* for guitar and orchestra, and Barber's Violin Concerto. Other twentieth-century composers had their cake and ate it, writing concertos that combined delicacy and showmanship, slipping from one to the other as the mood took them. Good samples are Ravel's Piano Concerto in G, Prokofiev's Violin Concerto No. 1 and Ibert's cheerful but death-defyingly difficult Flute Concerto.

FOR MORE CONCERTOS   See Pages 4, 17, 23, 26, 50, 69, 88, 104, 115, 155, 167, 208.

COPLAND
Rodeo: Four Dance Episodes

Rodeo, a cowboy ballet, was the hit of the 1942 New York season, and the Four Dance Episodes turn some of the best numbers into a rollicking orchestral suite. We begin with a swaggering 'Buckaroo Holiday', all clinking spurs and oompah tunes as the cowboys strut their stuff on the parade that begins the Saturday afternoon rodeo. 'Corral Nocturne' is a quiet interlude, based on a wistful slow tune in five-beat time. 'Saturday Night Waltz' is a restrained, dainty affair, more flirting than dancing – but everything changes with 'Hoedown', a thigh-slappin', fiddle-scrapin', banjo-twangin' finale to bring the house down.

RODEO   *Rodeo* tells the story of how a simple cowgirl goes to the ball, outsmarting a group of big-city missies to get her man. Copland uses real cowboy tunes, and the ballet is as stuffed with cowpokes, saloon-bar showdowns and barn dances as even the most ornery Wild West fan could ask. *Rodeo* took twenty-two curtain-calls at its first performance, and has headed the 'Most Wanted' list in ballet theatres ever since.

COPLAND   Aaron Copland (1900–90), the son of a Brooklyn department store owner, began studying music seriously only in his late teens. He started to win prizes in his mid-twenties and subsequently made his living equally as composer, pianist and conductor. Few twentieth-century 'serious' composers have had such huge success both with highbrow critics and with ordinary music-lovers. It must feel strange to write classical 'standard' after 'standard' – but that (at least from 1935 onwards) is exactly what Copland did.

COPLAND'S MUSIC   Until his mid-thirties Copland wrote spiky, avant-garde music that was admired more than it was liked. Then he decided to change his style, to write concert music of high quality but which everyone could enjoy. The result was a dozen of the century's best-loved works, whose rangy tunes and clean-scrubbed scoring have been imitated by every film and TV composer since. *Jaws*, *Dallas*, *The Magnificent Seven*, *Indiana Jones* – all began with Copland's *Fanfare for the Common Man* – *El Salón México*, *Appalachian Spring* and Symphony No. 3, which run rings round them for colour and quality.

NOW TRY Copland, *Billy the Kid*; *Appalachian Spring*. Grofé, *Grand Canyon* Suite. Piston, *The Incredible Flutist*.

DEBUSSY
Clair de Lune

Clair de lune is a musical impression of moonlight.
Debussy wrote it for piano solo, and it still sounds best that
way, though arrangements exist for string orchestra, organ,
harp, even jazz band and vocal group.

The music starts with serene, slow-moving blocks of
sound, as if we were seeing the moon high in a dark night
sky. Then – as the moon seems slowly to move across the sky
– the same music is repeated, still serene but broken down
into wisps and fragments of sound. Sharp, high harmonies
suggest the glint of moonbeams. A calm tune appears, with a
rippling accompaniment, as if clouds were passing across
the moon. Gradually everything quietens again, and we hear
once more the still sounds of the opening, with one last
cloud-ripple as the piece dies away to silence.

ENDYMION   This piece shares its mood with the story of
Endymion in Greek myth. The moon goddess, riding across
the sky, caught sight of a beautiful shepherd, Endymion,
sleeping on the hills below. Filled with passion, she stepped
down to earth to seduce him. But her radiance scorched his
mortal flesh and he withered and died before her eyes. Sadly,
she resumed her lonely journey, and has kept aloof from
mortals ever since.

PLAYING FOR DEBUSSY   Maurice Dumenis, as a piano
student, went one afternoon to play for Debussy. He later
wrote: 'The room was dimly lit through rich curtains,
whose long, blue-grey folds matched the thick carpet.
Antique furniture; a low, marble-topped table, covered
with small objects of crystal, jade or gold. Debussy

said little, and seemed somehow absent, his dark eyes fixed on distant horizons. He held a cigarette between his fingers, and kept depositing the ash carefully in a small china tray. As I played, I sensed him behind me, pacing the gorgeous Oriental rugs, smoking. About "Clair de lune", he said that the left-hand music should be flowing, mellow, drowning in pedal, as if played by a harp against a background of strings ...'

NOW TRY   Other Debussy piano works: 'The Girl With Flaxen Hair' (*Preludes*, Book I No. 8); 'The Drowned Cathedral' (*Preludes*, Book I No. 10). Similar pieces by others: Satie, *Gymnopédie* No. 1. Rachmaninov, *Vocalise*. Fauré, *Pavane*.

DEBUSSY
Prélude à l'après-midi d'un faune

Debussy wrote some of the most sensuous, evocative orchestral music ever composed. *Prélude à l'après-midi d'un faune* ('Prelude to a Faun's Afternoon') is a sound-picture of an adolescent faun (magical creature, half-boy, half-goat) lying in a dappled wood on a summer afternoon. Idly, he watches nymphs playing, tries half-heartedly to catch them, dreams erotic dreams, returns to his doze. The music starts with a sleepy flute solo, which gradually grows into a long tune on horn and strings, accompanied by melting, dreamlike harmonies. There are tiny flurries of busyness, but on the whole the music keeps up its languorous, erotic slowness from first to last.

In 1909 *L'après-midi* was made into one of the sultriest ballets of the century. The great dancer Nijinsky played the faun, in a costume which made him look like a naked youth dappled with forest leaves. The ballet caused a scandal, and made Nijinsky's name – hardly surprising, not just because of the costume but because the music is so gloriously seductive – naughty but very, very nice.

DEBUSSY   Claude Debussy's (1862–1918) early ambitions were to be a concert pianist, and he started composing seriously only in his thirties. He wrote songs, and a huge amount of piano music, collections of short pieces with titles like paintings: 'Goldfish', 'The Girl With Flaxen Hair', 'Fireworks', 'Gardens in the Rain'. Even his large-scale works for orchestra have pictorial titles: *The Sea*, *Nocturnes*, *Images*. He explored new kinds of harmony, and was fond of mixing Western 'classical' ideas with those of Far Eastern music and his other great enthusiasm, jazz.

DEBUSSY AND THE IMPRESSIONISTS   As a student in Paris, Debussy knew several Impressionist painters, including Monet, Manet, Renoir and Degas. Rather than show photo-like representations of reality, their paintings gave impressions conveying an idea of what the artist felt and saw, and awakening emotion in the spectators. Debussy's music is 'impressionist' in a similar way: sound-images conjuring up sights, sounds and feelings.

NOW TRY   Debussy, 'Ibéria' (from *Images*: orchestral impressions of sunny Spain); *Jeux* (another ballet written for Nijinsky, about a young man and two young women flirting over a game of tennis). Delius, *The Walk to the Paradise Garden*. Ravel, *Pavane pour une infante défunte*. Liadov, *The Enchanted Lake*. Falla, 'Miller's Dance' (from *The Three-cornered Hat*).

DELIBES
'Flower Duet' from *Lakmé*

Lakmé and her maid sing about a beautiful garden, a haven of peace where jasmine and roses, twining white on pink, bless the air with scent.

To create this effect in sound, Delibes has two voices in close harmony, rising and falling like flower petals trembling in the breeze. Nothing mars the beauty of the sound – this is the piece for which the phrase 'liquid harmony' might have been coined, and it's one of the best-loved of all classical music numbers, a joy to millions.

L AKMÉ The story is set in nineteenth-century India. Lakmé's father is a temple priest at odds with the British authorities. Gerald, a young officer, meets and falls in love with Lakmé – and her father stabs him. Lakmé nurses him, and asks him to drink from a spring of eternal love. He does so, but she knows that he is torn between love for her and for his regiment, which is to leave the next day. She solves his dilemma by taking poison, and dies in his arms.

D ELIBES Léo Delibes (1836–91) worked as a church organist on Sundays and during the week as theatrical composer and rehearsal pianist. Although, mysteriously, his name is now hardly known, his music is among the most popular in the world. We may, for example, have never heard of *Sylvia* and *Coppélia*, but if we don't recognize their music as soon as we hear it, we must have been living on a desert island.

T HE MYSTIC EAST *Lakmé* is one of dozens of nineteenth-century pieces set in the mysterious Orient. In days before mass travel, all people knew of 'distant parts' was an

exotic mixture of the charming and the sinister. In Saint-
Saëns's *Samson and Delilah*, Delilah is portrayed as the
Eastern temptress to end them all. Bizet's *The Pearl Fishers*
must be the only Western opera ever set in Indonesia.
Puccini's *Madame Butterfly* is set in a fantasy Japan. Even
when works were located nearer home, for example Bizet's
Carmen, Eastern exoticism was allowed full play. French
composers were especially good at this, and none was better
than Delibes.

NOW TRY Delibes, 'Bell Song' (from *Lakmé*); Suite,
Coppélia. Bizet, 'Au fond du temple saint' (from *The
Pearl Fishers*). Canteloube, 'Baïléro' (from *Songs of the
Auvergne*).

DVOŘÁK
Slavonic Dance Op. 46 No. 8

Crashing chords begin this whirling gypsy dance. The
rhythm is actually a fast waltz, but the speed is so hectic that
you hear not three-in-a-bar (as usual with a waltz) but one-
in-a-bar. Dvořák then tricks the ear further by 'swinging'
the beats, so that they come when we're least expecting
them, producing a feeling of exhilaration and headlong
energy. The piece tantalizes by slowing down for a few
seconds at a time, as if the music were running out of steam,
then picking up pace and rushing off, exuberant as ever. The
tunes are so fresh and the rhythm is so catchy that you can
hear the surprises in this music time and again, and still they
should make you smile.

DVOŘÁK   Antonín Dvořák (1841–1904), a viola player in
the orchestra of the Prague National Theatre, was an
unassuming, happy man, devoted to his family and his

hobbies: pigeon-breeding and steam-engine spotting. His music is tuneful, brilliantly written for players and singers, and three-handkerchief romantic – serene one minute and sobbing its heart out the next. Some composers are admired, others beloved; Dvořák leads the second group.

SLAVONIC DANCES   In the 1850s Brahms published sets of *Hungarian Dances* for piano duet: arrangements and original pieces in gypsy style. They were hugely popular, and many composers, including Dvořák, set out to follow suit. Greatly daring – he regarded Brahms as some kind of musical god – Dvořák sent him the first set of *Slavonic Dances*, and was overjoyed when Brahms arranged for his own publisher to bring them out: a tremendous boost to Dvořák's reputation. Originally the *Dances* were for two players at one piano (a favourite kind of music with the nineteenth-century middle class), but Dvořák later arranged them for orchestra, with even greater success. His delight was complete when Brahms asked him to do the same for his own *Hungarian Dances* – an almost unheard-of compliment.

NOW TRY   Dvořák wrote sixteen *Slavonic Dances* altogether, and these are considered some of music's most unfailing joys. Similar pieces are his *Legends*, Three Slavonic Rhapsodies Nos. 1–3 and the effervescent *Scherzo capriccioso*. Good follow-ups by others: Brahms, Hungarian Dances. Weinberger, Polka and Fugue from *Schwanda the Bagpiper*. Enescu, *Romanian Rhapsodies* Nos. 1 and 2.

DVOŘÁK
Symphony No. 9, 'New World'

Dvořák wrote this symphony in the US – hence the nickname. But apart from the slow movement (in the style of a spiritual), the music prefers the sounds of the Old World to the New. Most of its tunes are in the style of Dvořák's beloved Bohemian folk music, and it has the bouncy rhythms and gorgeous orchestral writing that give all his music its feeling of energetic happiness.

The first movement's solemn introduction leads to a fast section whose main theme rises and falls like waves rippling across the sea. A perky, folk-song-like theme provides chattering contrast to the main melody's mock solemnity. The slow movement begins with a tune that has been used by advertisers to sell 'traditional' English bread, cheese, clothes, houses and even cider. The third movement is a fast three-time dance (featuring that Cinderella instrument the triangle), and the symphony ends with a combination of march and dance, a whole village holiday caught in sound.

DVOŘÁK'S MUSIC Dvořák's admiration for Brahms led him to write symphonies, sonatas, string quartets and other 'big' works. But his bubbly humour and his ear for catchy tunes and rhythms make grandeur, in his music, take a decided second place. If Brahms's works are cathedrals of sound, Dvořák's are flower-filled country churches.

DVOŘÁK IN THE US In 1892 Dvořák was invited to head a New York Conservatory of Music. He was entranced by America, especially its cocktails (he tried a record nineteen of them on the first day ashore), the pigeon house at the Bronx Zoo and the steamships on the Hudson river.

He claimed that every musician in the States was a genius, and his hosts responded by lionizing him. Although he missed Bohemia, and worried about his daughters picking up Yankee slang, the years he spent in the USA were three of the happiest of his life.

EXPLORING DVOŘÁK   From Dvořák's shorter works, we recommend the Humoresque (in its day one of the best-known pieces of the century), the beautiful song 'Silent Woods' and the rumbustious *Carnival* Overture. From his longer works we recommend the *Symphonic Variations* and Symphony No. 8 for orchestra, the *Stabat mater* for choir and orchestra and the Cello Concerto, an all-time favourite.

NOW TRY   Dvořák, Symphony No. 8. Borodin, Symphony No. 2. Schubert, Symphony No. 8, the 'Unfinished'.

EARLY MUSIC

'Early music' is record-catalogue shorthand for works produced in Europe between the eleventh and sixteenth centuries. Before the eleventh century music was not written down, and by the end of the sixteenth century we reach, so to speak, the musical mainstream.

The music of this time is delightful and approachable, but takes some tracking down. Only the grandest works (church music, say, or festive pieces for royal weddings) were fully written out. Other kinds of music survive in haphazard collections, and have to be 'realized' (reconstructed) before they can be performed today. Until about thirty years ago this fact kept early music in a kind of scholarly attic; it is only recently that specialist groups have taken it up and made it popular. Performing early music is a main branch of the 'authentic' movement in music: re-creating, so far as is possible, the original sound of each piece as its first audiences would have heard it.

For the listener, choosing what to hear can be quite a problem. Many pieces are short, and many have no named composer. Concerts and recordings are often anthologies of pieces, with dozens of composers represented. One of the simplest ways to start, therefore, is to sample the recordings of a particular early music group (we recommend the King's Consort, the Praetorius Ensemble and the Early Music Group of London), and branch out from there.

CHURCH MUSIC

More church music survives than any other kind, and it is generally far grander. Most of it was written for one or other of the great European Churches, and the composers tried to produce sound-equivalents for the soaring intricacies of the architecture, worshipping God in music as the builders had in stone. Works (generally with Latin texts) range from short anthems to Mass settings lasting half an hour or more. Good composers to try: Dufay (whose works are the shortest and jolliest), Josquin Despres (whose works are the most sensuous), Palestrina (most intricate), and Victoria (most sumptuous).

INSTRUMENTAL MUSIC

There are two kinds of early instrumental music. For aristocratic players and listeners, composers developed elaborate pieces for such instruments as keyboard or lute, often in the form of fantasias (free-form pieces of counterpoint) or variation-sets. Patrons were fond of variation-sets using popular tunes, where each variation was more far-fetched and virtuosic than the last. (Good composers to try: Byrd, Farnaby, Frescobaldi, Swee-linck.) Ordinary people's music, however, written mainly for dancing, was seldom preserved and not much of it survives. The pieces that do are absolutely delightful – among the most ear-catching of all early music sounds. (Good composers to try: Susato, Praetorius.)

VOCAL MUSIC

Solo songs and songs for vocal ensembles (four, five or more solo voices) were also enjoyed during this period. Often, the same songs were arranged for both formats. They ranged from simple, verse-and-chorus numbers (French composers were especially good at these – try Passereau's 'Il est bel et bon') to more elaborate, emotionally complex works. Examples of the second kind are lute-songs, usually exploring tragic or philoso-phical moods (Dowland's are some of the finest) and madrigals (songs for ensemble; good composers to try are the Englishmen Wilbye, Morley and Gibbons, and the finest of all madrigal composers, the Italian Monteverdi).

WILLIAM BYRD (1542–1623)

Byrd wrote church music (mainly anthems), madrigals, solo songs and instrumental works. Recommended: Mass for Five Voices; keyboard works (mostly for virginals).

CLAUDIO MONTEVERDI (1567–1643)
Monteverdi wrote operas, madrigals and church music.
Recommended: Madrigals Book 2; *Vespers of 1610*
(written for St Mark's, Venice); opera *Orfeo*.

GIOVANNI PIERLUIGI DA PALESTRINA (1525–94)
Palestrina wrote sacred music, most of it for unaccompanied choir, for the churches of St John Lateran and
Santa Maria Maggiore in Rome. His works include
ninety-four masses, which are among the great glories
of Western music. Recommended: *Stabat mater*;
Missa Papae Marcelli.

START HERE (works to whet the appetite)
Instrumental: Any virginals pieces by Byrd or
Farnaby. Any dance pieces by Susato or Praetorius;
Sweelinck, *Mein Junges Leben Hat Ein' End* (organ
solo); Gabrieli, *Sonata pian e forte* (brass ensemble).
Vocal: Dowland, 'In Darkness Let Me Dwell'; 'Fine
Knacks for Ladies' (lute-songs); Gibbons, 'The Silver
Swan' (madrigal); Lassus, 'Matona, mia cara' (madri-
gal); Monteverdi, 'Chiome d'oro' (madrigal).
Choral: Tallis, 'Spem in alium' (church motet);
Victoria, 'O magnum mysterium' (motet); Josquin,
Missa Pange Lingua (mass).

ELGAR
'Enigma' Variations

Elgar called the theme of these fourteen variations
'Enigma', and refused to explain. (He said it was a tune that
fitted another well-known tune, but did not identify it.)
Each variation is a sound-picture of one of Elgar's family or

friends and is in different mood and style: his publisher
thinks noble thoughts; a dog splashes in the river during a
towpath walk; a girl languishes and simpers; and so on. The
effect is like being at a party, with your host (Elgar) at your
elbow to guide your impression of the people you meet.

In the fourteenth variation Elgar turns the spotlight on
himself, closing the set with a swaggering movement
undercut by worried flurries and runs in wind and strings.
This variation also quotes from an overture ('Calm Sea and
Prosperous Voyage') by Mendelssohn. Another mystery. Is
this a coded reference to some secret in Elgar's life? He
puffs his pipe, looks us in the eye and invites us to guess.

ELGAR   Edward Elgar (1857–1934) worked as a violinist,
organist and conductor of amateur orchestras (including
that of the local lunatic asylum) in provincial Worcester,
until the 'Enigma' Variations brought him worldwide fame.
He became England's leading composer, an Establishment
figure loaded with honours and commissioned to write big
works for important national occasions. Someone said that
he was 'as British as John Bull'; Elgar ruefully wrote that
he'd been far happier giving violin lessons and selling sheet
music in Worcester.

ELGAR AND THE GRAMOPHONE   Elgar was one of the
first big 'names' people turned to when recording was
introduced, and he made dozens of records of his own music.
Photos survive of brilliantine-haired, morning-suited
players crowding to scrape or blow into the huge cardboard
tubes that were the forerunners of microphones, with Elgar,
a small, dapper figure, standing somewhat forlornly with
his baton well out of range. But the performances are
fascinating – not least the one of his Violin Concerto he
made with the sixteen-year-old Yehudi Menuhin. (He

rehearsed for ten minutes with the boy before saying, 'Oh, that's enough. Let's go to the races.')

Now TRY Elgar, *Cockaigne* Overture; *Nursery* Suite. Brahms, Variations on a Theme by Haydn. Richard Strauss, *Don Quixote*.

ELGAR
Cello Concerto

Solo cellos are easily swamped by full orchestral sound, and the score of Elgar's concerto therefore contains more empty space than notes; this means that every note played is essential, with no room for waste. The concerto is as delicate as chamber music.

Whether Elgar's scoring helped to create the concerto's mood, or the mood led to the scoring, they fit miraculously. Few other works match this concerto's air of wistful, nostalgic sadness. The tone is set in the first movement. After a few moments of assertion from the cello, a wispy, meandering tune begins, as if someone were aimlessly humming. A second, more athletic theme breaks in, before wispiness returns, leading directly to the second movement. This is a quiet scamper of cello notes interrupted by one of the shortest 'big tunes' ever written: nine notes, in this ethereal context as startling as if someone had yelled in church.

The slow movement, the heart of the concerto, seems designed specifically to break your heart. For years this concerto was associated with the cellist Jacqueline du Pré, who died of multiple sclerosis – which makes hearing it, especially her recording, even more poignant. The last movement is a kind of subdued march with agile cello passages, but at the end the (miniature) 'big tune' returns, as if to show up the hollowness of all the pomp we've just been hearing.

EDWARDIAN ELGAR People who knew nothing of Elgar but 'Land of Hope and Glory' might imagine him as a figure of typically Edwardian self-confidence and swagger, the British Empire personified. In fact, whenever he catches that mood in his music, he balances it with a melancholic nostalgia that seems to hint at private, unreachable sorrow. This is his personal voice, and though it's missing from 'Land of Hope and Glory', it gives his bigger works, such as this concerto, their 'Elgarness'. Nowadays people suggest that the whole English Edwardian Age was like this: a kind of Indian summer of Victorian values that everyone knew were doomed in a world of flappers, jazz and Fascism. If that's so, Elgar is, precisely, the Edwardian to end them all.

NOW TRY Elgar, Introduction and Allegro; *Falstaff*. Dvořák, Cello Concerto. Tchaikovsky, *Variations on a Rococo Theme*. Walton, Viola Concerto.

FALLA
Dances from *The Three-cornered Hat*

The Three-cornered Hat is that rare thing in ballet, a sexy farce. A buffoon of an official (the hat is his badge of office) fancies the wife of a fanatically jealous miller. He has the miller arrested to clear the way for love, and the miller's wife dances seductively to lead him on, tumbles him in the river, then partly undresses him to dry him – at which point the miller comes back home ...

Falla's score is recorded complete (and is well worth exploring), but he made a separate suite of three short dances. They take us straight to the heart of sunny Spain. The Neighbours' Dance is graceful and seductive (the women swaying while the lip-smacking official spies and drools). The Miller's Dance alternates a wailing, Moorish tune and ever-quickening, flamenco stamping. The Final Dance is a *jota*: a whirling dance in three-time, with everyone mocking the soaked official as the orchestra supplies guitar-like strumming and clacking castanets. The music gets faster and faster, a rush of sound as heady as a cocktail. This may be picture-postcard Spain, but it sets every foot tapping in even the solemnest concert hall.

THE RUSSIAN BALLET   Falla wrote *The Three-cornered Hat* in 1919 for Diaghilev's Russian Ballet company (already known for such exotic dazzlers as *Sheherazade* and *The Firebird*). His collaborators included three of the century's most glittering theatre talents: Picasso designed the ballet (basing it on pictures by Goya, no less); Massine did the choreography – and conceived the part of the Miller, alternately brooding and stupendously athletic, for himself; and the wife was played by Karsavina, the most elfin, but most seductive, of all Diaghilev's harem of leading ladies.

FALLA   Manuel de Falla (1876–1946) was fascinated by Andalusian folk music, with its Arab-inspired tunes and its stiff-backed, rhythmic flamenco dances, named for the flamingoes whose flounce and strut they imitate. He wrote this kind of local colour into songs, piano pieces, choral works, concertos, and above all three gorgeous stage works: *The Three-cornered Hat*, *Love the Magician* and *La vida breve* ('Life is Short').

Now try Falla, 'Ritual Fire Dance' (from *Love the Magician*; Chabrier, *España*. Albéniz, *Iberia* (ballet version).

FAURÉ
Pavane

The pavane was originally a sixteenth-century European court dance. Intended for people who would be wearing elaborate, heavy clothes, it combined a minimum of brisk movement with a maximum of graceful bowing and curtseying and refined hand-touching. Fauré was fascinated by this kind of elegance, as shown in court pictures by such artists as Watteau (court painter to Louis XIV) – and his orchestral pavane seeks to catch a similar mood.

The music begins with a dainty, melancholy flute tune, sounding almost too watery to live. But its slightness is deceptive: it is the backbone of the whole piece. Each time it is repeated (and it often is), Fauré adds new harmonies, takes it in different directions, extends it and rescores it, so that the pavane gathers energy as it proceeds. The music reaches a climax of loud horn calls, even a discord or two. Then it quietens down and the dance begins again, unwinding gradually until it dies away to silence.

FAURÉ Gabriel Fauré (1845–1924) was a composition professor, and taught some of the best-known French composers of the century. His own works include songs (at which he was a master), piano suites, sonatas, a string quartet and other large pieces. But he also had the knack of writing small-scale, tuneful music that instantly captured a mood or set a scene. He composed incidental music for plays, and several short orchestral works like this pavane: water-colours in sound.

WHIM OF STEEL   Fauré was a mild-mannered man, but
when the chips were down he always got his way. He waited
for years to be appointed head of the Paris Conservatoire,
his path being continually blocked by people who thought
him too 'lightweight' for the job. He was finally appointed
in 1905, when he was sixty. Some opponents still remained,
and Fauré went quietly round, talking gently to them one
by one, after which each found a reason to resign. 'He's just
like Robespierre,' one wit muttered. 'Give us this day our
daily head . . .'

NOW TRY   Fauré, *Masques et bergamasques* Suite; *Dolly*
Suite; song 'Après un rêve' (also scored as an instrumental
solo). Ravel, *Pavane pour une infante défunte*. Debussy,
Petite Suite.

FAURÉ
Requiem

For centuries, composers have used the text of the Requiem
Mass for some of their largest, grandest works. It offers
wonderful opportunities for musical contrast: an opening
lament followed by a picture of the Day of Judgement,
then subdued prayers for mercy. Requiems are also more
public, less liturgical affairs than ordinary masses, and lavish
music perhaps seems less out of place.

Fauré was a reticent composer, not given to blaring
drama or heart-on-sleeve supplication. (Verdi's *Requiem* is
the work for that). He wrote for comparatively small forces:
choir, two soloists, organ and string orchestra, about fifty
performers altogether. (Berlioz thought a thousand the
ideal number for his *Requiem*.) The work's intimate scale
draws the listener's concentration, points up the detail and

meaning of what is being sung. The tension is so focused that one 'unusual' harmony, a single moment's unexpectedness, can send shivers down the spine. The *Requiem* also boasts one of the great hit tunes for boy soprano: 'Pie Jesu', a prayer of innocence and entreaty which soars to the heights and tears the listener's heart.

FAURÉ AND THE CHURCH   Not satisfied with a full-time teaching job and his prolific composition, Fauré the workaholic also found time to be organist and choirmaster at the Madeleine, one of Paris's grandest churches. As well as the *Requiem*, he wrote a handful of other works for his choir there, and they have a sureness of touch, an instinct for what voices can do, which only 'insiders' seem to manage. (You can hear this in the music. Mozart's church music, for example – he was not a strong believer – is the work of a great composer who just happens to write for the Church. Fauré's is that of a devout Christian offering his skill to his God: a very different effect.)

EXPLORING FAURÉ   From Fauré's lighter works, we recommend the *Masques et bergamasques* Suite and the *Sicilienne* for cello and piano. From his more serious works, we recommend Sonata No. 2 for violin and piano, the song cycle *L'Horizon chimérique* and the coolly beautiful choral work 'Ave Maria', Op. 67 No. 2.

NOW TRY   Fauré, 'Salve regina', Op. 67 No. 1; 'Tantum ergo'. Mendelssohn, 'Hear My Prayer' (including treble solo 'O, for the Wings of a Dove'. Allegri, *Miserere*. Vaughan Williams, *Serenade to Music*.

GERSHWIN
Porgy and Bess

Porgy and Bess is part grand opera, part musical. An opera with show-tunes instead of arias, it is set among black tenement-dwellers in 1920s Carolina, and tells of the love of crippled Porgy for Bess, the girlfriend of Crown, who is in hiding for murder.

The vigorous, complicated plot involves fights, police raids, crap games, a funeral wake, a picnic and a prayer-meeting. The music stirs together Puccini-like opera, jazz, spiritual, and above all a string of unforgettable big numbers: 'Summer Time', 'I Got Plenty of Nothing', 'It Ain't Necessarily So', 'A Woman Is a Sometime Thing' and the splendidly silly 'A Red-Headed Woman Makes a Choo-choo Jump Its Tracks'.

There are several ways to enjoy the opera. It is often staged, and has been filmed (with Sidney Poitier, Pearl Bailey and Sammy Davis Jnr) and recorded on video. All the great singers of the century, jazz and classical, have recorded individual songs. And there are two orchestral suites: pocket versions, so to speak, dispensing with voices but cramming all the tunes into about twenty minutes each. Gershwin called his own selection *Catfish Row*; Robert Russell Bennett called his *Porgy and Bess: Symphonic Picture*.

GERSHWIN   George Gershwin (1898–1937) wrote more 'standards' for Broadway and Hollywood than almost any other composer. His hit shows and films include *Lady Be Good*, *Strike Up the Band*, *Funny Face* and *Shall We Dance?*. But he was also interested in more 'mainstream', classical composition, and particularly in bridging the gap that then existed between 'symphonic' and 'popular' styles. Hence, among others, *Porgy and Bess*, the 'piano concerto in jazz' *Rhapsody in Blue* and *An American in Paris*, a piece for symphony orchestra which later became the basis for one of Gene Kelly's most balletic films.

NOW TRY Gershwin songs: 'I Got Rhythm'; 'The Man I Love'; 'Lady Be Good'; 'The Way You Look Tonight'; ''S Wonderful'. Larger Gershwin works, apart from those mentioned: Cuban Overture; Variations on 'I Got Rhythm' (piano and orchestra); Piano Concerto. Follow-ups by others: Kern, *Showboat*. Loesser, *Guys and Dolls*. Bernstein, *West Side Story* and *Fancy Free*, and Rodgers, *Slaughter on Tenth Avenue* are good follow-ups to *An American in Paris*.

GLASS
Akhnaten

Glass's theatre-piece *Akhnaten* is a dazzle of dance, movement and light all set to a hypnotic, exotic score. It tells the life of the misshapen dreamer Akhnaten, who became Pharaoh of Egypt some 3500 years ago, of his love for his beautiful wife Nefertiti, and of his doomed attempts to convert Egypt from its bloody, multi-god religion to a visionary, new faith worshipping one God only, the Sun.

The man-woman Akhnaten is played by a counter-tenor, whose unearthly arias colour the entire score. The words (partly in ancient Egyptian) include a Hymn to the Sun by the real-life Akhnaten: the world's earliest surviving piece of music. Design is based on relics in the Cairo Museum. As someone said, the opera is 'flesh-and-blood archaeology'. It's also one of the century's weirdest theatre works, and seeing

it on stage or on video or laserdisc is essential for the full
effect – though sound recordings do make a useful entry-
point to Glass's unique sound-world.

GLASS   Philip Glass (born 1937) devised a new kind of
'minimalist' music, using endless tiny changes in a
continuously repeated rhythm. Tunes and harmony are
stripped down to basics, and everything depends on the zen-
like, hypnotic rhythmic blur. Glass tours with his own
ensemble, and their following is as large as any rock group's.
He also writes big-scale operas: *Akhnaten* is the third part of
a trilogy whose other operas centre on Einstein and Gandhi.

MINIMALISM   Minimalism is a concept applied in all the
arts. The artist takes a single creative component – one
shape or colour in painting; one idea or word in poetry; one
rhythm or melody in music – and focuses our attention on
it. The Russian minimalist Kasimir Malevich painted white
squares on white canvas; a haiku poem distils an entire
experience into seventeen syllables; Glass's works circle
round many-times-repeated note patterns. The idea is not
to batter us with input (as non-minimalist art does), but for
us to empty our minds and focus our concentration, as
happens in meditation.

NOW TRY   Glass, *Low* Symphony (transforming a song
by David Bowie); *Glassworks* (splendid CD anthology);
Satyagraha (Gandhi opera, transforming Indian musical
styles). Adams, 'The Chairman Dances' (from *Nixon in
China*; Reich, *Phase Patterns for Four Organs*.

GÓRECKI
Symphony No. 3

Górecki based this 'Symphony of Sorrowful Songs' on the idea of the music of the spheres, and began it thirty years after the Second World War, completing it in 1976. His idea was that the Nazi treatment of Jews was against nature, typical of the way humans distort universal harmony. We can recover harmony by meditation, by contemplation – and when we do, the reward is serenity.

The symphony is in two halves, each lasting about twenty-five minutes. The first begins with a deep, slow melody which dozens of string voices pick up and echo, one after another, to create a vast vault of sound. At its peak, a solo voice sings Mary's cry for help to her son Jesus, taken from a medieval manuscript – and then the music reverses its flow, unpeeling layer by layer until we reach the starting-point again.

In the second half, Górecki blurs pairs of enormous chords in and out of one another like the grinding of tectonic plates. The effect is vast, eternal – and edgy. The voice sings twice: a prayer to the Virgin Mary (the words of which were scrawled on a wall in the Zakopane Gestapo headquarters in 1944), and a lament for a lost child. As this last song ends, on the words 'Birds, sing for him; flowers bloom for him; let him sleep in peace', the symphony reaches a radiant, unified chord: universal harmony, restored.

MUSIC OF THE SPHERES   Pythagoras (sixth century BC) held that the universe was controlled by numbers and the relationships between them. Perfection happened when the relationships were correct; their disturbance led to anarchy.

In the heavens, Pythagoras believed, each planet followed its own fixed path, emitting its own unique sound. The sounds blended to make the 'music of the spheres'. If the planets followed correct courses, universal harmony resulted. But if just one sphere wandered, it created a jangle which led to misery, war and death.

In recent years, Górecki and other composers have blended this idea with Eastern teachings about timelessness and meditation. Their music is an aid to self-discovery: one should surrender to it as if to a mantra or other spiritual exercise.

Now try Górecki, Symphony No. 2; *Old Polish Music*. Tavener, *The Protecting Veil*. Tippett, *A Child of Our Time*. Honegger, Symphony No. 2.

GOUNOD
Faust

Gounod was the Andrew Lloyd Webber of his day (the 1860s), and *Faust* was his *Joseph and the Amazing Technicolor Dreamcoat*. An 1880s music critic reckoned that in one week alone there were forty-seven different performances of *Faust* within cab-range of central London, and the same was true throughout Europe and the US.

To be as famous as this, an opera needs a cast-iron story and brilliant tunes. Faust's story gives a new twist to a familiar tale, and its music seeps into your mind and stays there, exactly like Lloyd Webber's. Its biggest hits are the Soldiers' Chorus, the Flower Song and the ballet music (in which the Devil shows Faust a parade of history's most seductive women), but the opera is so crammed with delights that any chance to see it should be snatched without hesitation.

THE STORY   Faust, a medieval alchemist, conjures up a swashbuckling gentleman: Mephistopheles, the Devil. In exchange for his soul, Mephistopheles offers him youth and the love of Marguerite – and then takes him on a whirlwind tour of the fleshpots, before leaving him to court Marguerite in her garden. Later, we see Marguerite in despair: she has borne Faust's child, and Faust has deserted her. (This is pure Victorian melodrama.) She prays for help. Meanwhile, during a witches' sabbath, Mephistopheles claims Faust's soul. Marguerite, now imprisoned for murdering her child, prays again; in a ray of light she is carried into heaven, and angels drive out Mephistopheles as the Easter Hymn announces that Faust's soul has been saved after all.

GOUNOD   Charles Gounod (1818–93) studied for the priesthood, but chose a career in music instead. *Faust* earned him millions, giving him the chance to write anything else he wanted: half a dozen other operas, church music (including six masses), two cheerful symphonies and a shelf-ful of songs.

NOW TRY   Gounod's other operas, even the best-known (*Romeo and Juliet*), are alas no match for *Faust*. For tunefulness and cheerfulness, the best follow-up is not vocal at all, but the delightful Little Symphony for Wind Instruments. His solo song 'Ave Maria' cheekily welds a soulful tune of his own to a keyboard piece by Bach. Good follow-ups to *Faust* by others are Delibes, *Sylvia* (for orchestral tunefulness) and Bizet, *Carmen* (for tunes and spectacle).

GRIEG
Peer Gynt Suite No. 1

Ibsen's play *Peer Gynt*, about a boaster snatched to a series of
unlikely supernatural adventures, is one of the peaks of
Scandinavian drama – and Grieg's incidental music, written
for an 1876 performance, includes some of the best-loved
movements in all classical music.

There are two *Peer Gynt* suites, and the first eclipses the
second both in popularity and in quality. It has four
movements. The first, 'Morning', begins with a flute tune
picked up and repeated by the rest of the orchestra – bright,
wide-eyed music, as if every cobweb of night had been
brushed aside. (In the play, Peer actually wakes up lost in the
Sahara, up a palm tree and being pelted with monkey-dung
– the music's charm is highly ironical. But that's another
story.)

The second movement, 'Åse's Death', is a set of
heartbreaking chords, written for the scene in which Peer
lulls his sick old mother not to sleep but to death, telling her
a nursery story. The third, 'Anitra's Dance', accompanies a
belly-dance performed for Peer by a desert maiden who may
or may not be a mirage, and the fourth, 'In the Hall of the
Mountain King', depicts the home of the trolls, who take
Peer hostage and try to steal his human identity. It starts
with a lumpish tune on bassoons, which is echoed by the
whole orchestra, louder and louder, until the mountain
collapses round Peer's ears.

SOLVEJG'S SONG In the play, despite the fantastic
adventures Peer undergoes – marrying troll-maidens,
talking to the Sphinx and the Devil, being made king of a
madhouse – his heart remains faithful to his youthful

sweetheart, Solvejg. At one point, in a vision, he sees her
singing a gentle, patient song as she looks after her goats on
the high mountainside above the fjord. Grieg's setting of
this song became a hit in its own right, and he and his wife,
who was a singer, used it as an encore in song recitals round
the world for over twenty-five years. It also exists as the last
movement of *Peer Gynt* Suite No. 2, and as a separate piece
for string orchestra.

NOW TRY Grieg, *Sigurd Jorsalfar* Suite; *Lyric* Suite
(orchestral version). Sibelius, *King Christian II* Suite.
Arnold, *English Dances*, Set 2.

GRIEG
Piano Concerto

Grieg's health was too poor for him to fulfil his ambition of
being a concert pianist. But he always yearned for the life,
and was particularly envious of Liszt. After hearing Liszt's
two concertos, he decided to try one of his own, and he
wrote this fiendishly difficult, virtuoso piece, one of the
beefiest in the repertoire. (He was slightly taken aback when
Liszt played the piano part perfectly the first time he saw it.)

Big-scale music was not really Grieg's speciality. He was a
master of songs, incidental music for plays and short mood
pieces for piano or for orchestra. For all its size, therefore,
his concerto contains no grand symphonic themes or ideas.
Instead, Rolls-Royce virtuosity is put to work on fresh,
simple harmonies and whistleable tunes. The shower of
piano notes that opens the work (endlessly parodied by
comedians: British readers may remember Morecambe and
Wise 'doing Grieg' with André Previn on a TV Christmas
show) leads into a first movement as bracing as a hill-walk,

followed by a melting slow movement (with wonderfully delicate duets for piano and flute), and a bouncy, folk-style finale. The toughest part of the whole concerto is the cadenza, a bravura solo display in the first movement. But that's the most serious Grieg allows himself to be; the rest is pure high spirits.

GRIEG'S CHARACTER Grieg was one of those people who are so innocent, so straightforward, so gentle, that you think they must be pulling your leg. Once, a friend praised one of his works, all but the last few bars which she said weren't up to the standard of the rest. 'Perfectly true,' said Grieg. 'When I wrote the rest I was inspired. But inspiration gave out there, so I had to make do without.' On another occasion, fishing with a friend, he scribbled a sudden inspiration on a piece of paper which then blew away into the water. Unseen by Grieg, the friend picked it out and began quietly whistling the tune. 'What's that?' asked Grieg. 'Just an idea I had,' answered the friend. 'Amazing,' said Grieg, straight-faced. 'I just had the same one.'

NOW TRY Grieg, Symphonic Dances; *Holberg* Suite. Tchaikovsky, Piano Concerto No. 1. Liszt, Piano Concerto No. 1.

HANDEL
'Arrival of the Queen of Sheba'

This piece of ceremonial bustle comes from Handel's oratorio *Solomon*, set in ancient Israel. Solomon, the Bible says, was so wise and God-fearing that the beautiful Queen of Sheba (from what is now Zimbabwe) set out to Jerusalem 'to prove him with hard questions'. This music shows us her exotic arrival: 'with a very great train, with camels that bore spices and very much gold and precious stones'.

Handel, fortunately for us, had neither camels, gold nor jewels. In an opera, he might have used all three, but oratorios, being based on the Bible, were serious affairs, and were not staged. He was forced to show pomp and ceremony in the music alone. The strings fizz and chatter, and oboes play busy fanfares. Everything is brisk, bright and cheerful: three minutes of jollity before the 'hard questions' start. The rest of *Solomon* is rarely heard, but this piece has become a classical lollipop, recorded not only by strings and oboes, but in arrangements for piano, organ, and even (with death-defying virtuosity) by the unaccompanied voices of Swingle II.

HANDEL George Frederic Handel (1685–1759) was denied music as a boy: his parents wanted him to be a lawyer. However – and there may be a lesson for all parents here – family opposition redoubled his determination, and he practised the violin and harpsichord secretly in the attic. At eighteen he left home to make a career as player and opera composer – and by twenty-one he was famous. In 1710 he settled in London, and spent the rest of his life there as one of the most lionized composers of the age.

HANDEL'S TEMPER Handel's rehearsals were famous for his outbursts. People claimed that he threw scores, his wig, even chairs, at musicians who displeased him. His grumbling and his bluntness were notorious. One tenor grew so cross that he said, 'Unless you mend your ways, Mr Handel, I'll jump on your harpsichord and smash it.' 'Please tell me when,' retorted Handel in the heavy accent that so delighted London. 'I'll sell tickets. More people vill pay to see you yump than to hear you zing.'

NOW TRY   Handel, *Music for the Royal Fireworks*; song 'O
Ruddier Than the Cherry' (from *Acis and Galatea*). Vivaldi,
'Autumn' (from *The Four Seasons*). Respighi, *The Birds*.

HANDEL
The Water Music

On 17 July 1717 (a still, warm day), King George I and a
bargeful of courtiers travelled down the Thames from
Whitehall to Chelsea, 'with music playing all the way'. They
dined at Chelsea, enjoyed more music, and returned upriver
at two in the morning to the accompaniment of yet another
concert. Handel provided the music for all this jollity –
according to some, following the royal barge in a second
boat, precariously conducting an enormous orchestra of
oboes, bassoons, trumpets, drums, strings and harpsichord.

The Water Music consists of two dozen short pieces. Some
are grand and pompous, making full use of drums and
trumpets. Others are dances, and as well as the expected
minuets, gavottes and jigs, Handel stirs in a few surprises,
including a couple of riotous hornpipes. Many of the
movements are well known on their own, and suites and
medleys of all kinds have been extracted from them. Handel
grouped the pieces in three suites (one for each part of the
royal celebration). Modern conductors either play the work
complete or make new suites of favourite movements.

HANDEL'S MUSIC   Most of Handel's music was composed for the theatre. He owned and managed his own
theatre in London (the King's, later managed by Sheridan,
on the site of the present Her Majesty's), and he produced a
new opera there each year for twenty years. (These were
chiefly based on stories from myth or history – Jupiter,

Xerxes, Julius Caesar, Tamerlane and a dozen others all strut
their amorous, murderous stuff.) When opera went out of
fashion in the 1740s, Handel took up a new musical form,
the Biblical oratorio, and wrote one or two of those each
year. He also composed sonatas, suites, church anthems
(including the famous 'Zadok the Priest', now traditional at
British coronations), and dozens of short harpsichord pieces
intended for his pupils (a good example is the set of
variations nicknamed 'The Harmonious Blacksmith'). Not
surprisingly for a theatre composer, his music is tuneful and
surefooted, but he was also a master of the grand manner:
even his slightest-seeming music can lift the heart.

NOW TRY   Handel, *Music for the Royal Fireworks*; Concerto
Grosso Op. 3 No. 1. Telemann, *Don Quixote* Suite. Bach,
Suite No. 3.

HANDEL
Messiah

Handel wrote *Messiah* in a fortnight, in a frenzy of
inspiration and devotion. It made a hit at its first London
performance – the King stood up for the 'Hallelujah'
Chorus, and everyone else followed suit – and it rapidly
became known all round the world. In nineteenth-century
Britain it was the best loved of all choral works, and a
tradition began of performing it at Christmas, wherever
possible with huge choirs (some of a thousand-plus) and
enormous orchestras, even though Handel's original needs
only about forty performers.

Messiah tells Jesus' story in recitatives (sung narration),
solo arias and choruses. Prophecies of Jesus' birth lead to the
Christmas story. The second section centres on Jesus' trial

and death, and the third is about his resurrection and second coming. For Christians, the words have profound significance; for non-believers, the work is a glorious concert of orchestral movement (like the so-called 'Pastoral Symphony' which depicts the Christmas shepherds), arias like 'Every Valley', 'He Shall Feed His Flock', 'I Know that My Redeemer Liveth' and 'The Trumpet Shall Sound', and a dozen mighty choruses including 'For Unto Us a Child Is Born', 'All We Like Sheep', 'Lift Up Your Heads' and of course 'Hallelujah' and 'Amen'.

'AUTHENTIC' HANDEL   Handel has benefited more than most from the 'authentic' movement: playing music of the past as closely as possible to the way the composer wrote it. This treatment makes his works seem trimmer and fleeter than the massive performances of the nineteenth and early twentieth centuries – and Handel-lovers seek out modern recordings and performances wherever possible. However, old-fashioned, big-scale Handel can still be found, and can be enthralling. An Albert Hall full of massed choirs 'doing' *Messiah*, or a symphony orchestra playing Hamilton Harty's arrangement of the *The Water Music*, are experiences both over the top and quite irresistible.

COMPOSING *MESSIAH*   For all Handel's gruffness, he was deeply sentimental and devout. While he was working on *Messiah*, the servant who took him his hot chocolate each morning often saw tears streaming down his cheeks and 'mixing with the ink', and a friend, visiting him while he was setting the words 'He was despised and rejected of men' found him sobbing so hard that he could hardly continue.

NOW TRY   Handel, *Acis and Galatea*. Haydn, *The Seasons*.
Walton, *Belshazzar's Feast* (twentieth-century music, but
equally vivid and engulfing).

HAYDN
Trumpet Concerto

For thousands of years – playable instruments have been
found in Egyptian pyramids – trumpets were among the
simplest of all musical instruments. Skilful performers could
play some dozen notes, and second-rank players less than
half a dozen. They were used chiefly for fanfares, and their
main uses were military. When trumpet-parts were called
for in eighteenth-century orchestras, players were often
drafted in from the nearest barracks, and the music written
for them, however effective, was very simple.

Not surprisingly, given these restrictions, trumpet
concertos were uncommon. But in the 1790s an 'improved'
trumpet was invented, with extra lengths of tubing opened
and closed by valves. This gave the player more notes, and
also made the instrument easier to play and more reliable. In
1796 the lead trumpeter in the Vienna Court Opera
orchestra bought such an instrument, and asked Haydn to
write him a concerto. Haydn took full advantage, treating
the trumpet like any other wind instrument – an oboe, say –
able to play tunes, runs and trills to the manner born. (The
only concessions are regular rests, so that the player can rest
his or her lip.)

Thanks to its perky main tune, the third movement of
concerto is often detached and heard as a separate brass
piece. But the other two parts are equally jolly: a lively
ovement, using keys no self-respecting trumpeter

had heard of until then, and a slow movement as limpid and soulful as any operatic aria.

HAYDN   As a youth Haydn was so poor that he had to work as manservant to an elderly colleague, being paid in cast-off clothes and lessons in harmony. It was not until he was twenty-five that he found proper employment, first as court composer to Count Morzin, and then for the Esterházy family, enormously wealthy, with whom he remained for thirty years, hiring and firing musicians, running an opera house, a church choir, a puppet theatre, an orchestra and chamber groups of all shapes and sizes, as well as writing hundreds of works: operas, chamber music, church pieces, and above all symphonies (over a hundred) and concertos for the court orchestra.

NOW TRY Haydn, Horn Concerto No. 2; *Sinfonia Concertante*. Mozart, Horn Concerto No. 4. Hummel, Trumpet Concerto.

HAYDN
Symphony No. 45, 'Farewell'

Working for the Esterházy family (see above) was like belonging to an exclusive club. Haydn knew his musicians intimately; he dealt with their money problems, acted as godfather to their children, played cards with them – and, above all, he wrote music for them, day in, day out. He built each player's skill and personality into the music. An oboe tune here, a high horn call there, a silky viola phrase – the Esterházy symphonies are like conversations between old, close friends.

In the 'Farewell' symphony, Haydn wrote for a reduced orchestra, the twenty or so musicians who joined the Prince at his hunting lodge. Two oboes (not the most proficient in the band, one deduces from their simple music), two horns (expert at long, high notes), a handful of strings. The small number of strings allowed Haydn to write more angular, savage music than for a larger ensemble, and perhaps this accounts for the gawkiness of the first movement, which sounds at times like waltzing wasps. The slow movement is a gentle meander, mainly for strings, and the minuet (as is often the case with with Haydn) parodies a rustic dance.

Confirmation that this was music for friends comes in the last movement, which starts with march-like bustle, then slows right down as the players begin a languid, exhausted-sounding piece. They try to gather energy, and fail. One by one, they put down their instruments and tiptoe out, until only two solo violins are left. This was a gentle hint from 'Papa' Haydn to their employer: the season had been long and the bandsmen needed a holiday. It worked – and Symphony No. 46 is there to show how refreshed they felt when they all came back.

HAYDN ON TOUR   By his mid-fifties, Haydn was lionized all over Europe and went on extensive tours. Even so, not everyone recognized him by sight. A 'neat little gentleman' called at Howell's music shop one day and asked to see piano music. Howell showed him the latest sonatas. 'I don't like these.' 'But, sir, they're Haydn's.' 'H'm. I wish you'd show me something better.' Howell, outraged, would have thrown him out if the stranger hadn't disclosed his true identity.

Now try   Haydn, Symphony No. 48 (written for a royal
visit, and full of whooping horns). Mozart, Symphony No.
29. Beethoven, Symphony No. 4.

HISTORY OF CLASSICAL MUSIC

BEGINNINGS

'Classical' music is the term used to describe European
art music of the last thousand years or so. It has nothing
to do with the Classical civilizations of ancient Greece
and Rome.

Most music is connected with either ceremony
(religious, state or private) or enjoyment. In the early
days (the Middle Ages), music in the West was no
different from anywhere else. Minstrels made up songs
and dance tunes, and the church used chants and hymns
– as happened everywhere in the world. The music was
not written down, but handed on from teacher to pupil,
learned by heart or improvised (made up on the spot). In
about the tenth century, however, the Christian authorities decided to standardize church music throughout
their vast domains, and a way was invented to write
music down.

Recording music on paper means that an archive is
created. Compositions are not confined to a small, local
area, but can be carried anywhere. Performers can read
and learn whatever music they like. As soon as a system
of writing music was invented, the art expanded in the
West a thousandfold. (Astonishingly, no other world
culture has ever felt the need to preserve its music in this
way.)

IN AND OUT OF CHURCH

Until about 1500, church music was the main area for composers, and there survives a huge number of settings of the Mass, the Psalms and other Bible passages. The songs and dances of ordinary life were generally learned or improvised as they had been before.

The expansion of non-church music began during the Renaissance, in the fourteenth and fifteenth centuries. It became customary for any self-respecting aristocrat to employ professionals who would compose and perform music for worship and for leisure – church pieces, 'table-music' (to eat by) and show-music (for listening). For each of these, composers developed special kinds of music. Concertos, for example, showed off instrumental skills, while cantatas and operas highlighted singers.

PUBLIC CONCERTS

From the 1650s onwards, many composers made a handsome secondary living by publishing their pieces, and their works were performed all over Europe. In the 1750s and beyond, the newly affluent merchants and manufacturers created by the Industrial Revolution felt that they were just as much entitled to musical entertainment as any aristocrat. Public concerts became a major source of income for composers and performers alike.

By 1800, three kinds of classical music were established. Church music ranged from simple hymns to elaborate Masses and Passions. Operas (now in specially built theatres) gave singers the chance to express every subtlety of emotion while demonstrating the beauty and agility of their voices. Instrumental music had by now evolved from simple dances to sonatas, suites, concertos and symphonies on the largest scale.

ON TO THE MILLENNIUM

In the first years of the nineteenth century, people began to regard some composers (for example Beethoven) and some performers (for example Paganini) not just as skilled craftsmen, but as geniuses whose achievements lesser mortals could only aspire to emulate. The idea grew that classical music was a 'high art', a pinnacle of human creation – and therefore that 'serious' musicians were somehow grander than people who dealt in such humbler creations as popular songs and dances. This gulf still, alas, affects some people's attitudes today.

The last great development for Western music was the invention of recording in the 1880s. Recordings were made of music of every kind, from classical to rock, from folk to jazz. Non-Western music affected Western styles; Western music spread throughout the world. Music, in short, was democratized, returned to the way it was before churchmen and aristocrats took it for their own – and our luck is that in the meantime, thanks to those wealthy, exclusive patrons, a vast library of treasures was created and can be universally enjoyed.

MAIN COMPOSERS IN THIS BOOK

Before 1700: Byrd, Monteverdi, Palestrina, Purcell.

1700–1800: Albinoni, Bach, Handel, Haydn, Mozart, Vivaldi.

1800–1900: Beethoven, Berlioz, Bizet, Borodin, Brahms, Chopin, Delibes, Dvořák, Fauré, Gounod,

Grieg, Leoncavallo, Liszt, Mahler, Massenet, Mendelssohn, Musorgsky, Offenbach, Paganini, Rimsky-Korsakov, Rossini, Saint-Saëns, Schubert, Schumann, Smetana, Johann Strauss, Sullivan, Tchaikovsky, Verdi, Wagner.

1900 to today: Barber, Bartók, Berg, Bernstein, Boulez, Britten, Copland, Debussy, Elgar, Falla, Gershwin, Glass, Górecki, Holst, Ives, Janáček, Khachaturian, Kodály, Messiaen, Nielsen, Orff, Puccini, Rachmaninov, Ravel, Respighi, Rodrigo, Schoenberg, Sibelius, Richard Strauss, Stravinsky, Tippett, Vaughan Williams, Walton, Webern.

HOLST
The Planets

When Holst composed *The Planets* in 1917, only seven planets had been identified. His idea was to write a musical picture of each planet's astrological associations. The idea is dry, but from it Holst made one of the most sumptuous orchestral show pieces composed this century.

The movements are:

'Mars, the Bringer of War': lurching discords lead to frantic trumpet-calls, an insistent rhythm and galloping, distracted fragments of tune.

'Venus, the Bringer of Peace': still, slow music, featuring a serene tune on woodwind and delicate harp harmonies.

'Mercury, the Winged Messenger': a breathless scamper, over almost as soon as it begins.

'Jupiter, the Bringer of Jollity': fast, festive music leads to a 'big tune' (later arranged as the hymn 'I Vow to Thee, My Country') – and then back to celebration.

'Saturn, the Bringer of Old Age': mysterious, halting chords, a sad procession. Holst was expert at writing 'frozen', emotionless music, and he seldom did it better than here.

'Uranus, the Magician': a 'magic' phrase on brass instruments is followed by lumpish cavortings; Uranus was clearly a buffoon as well as a conjurer.

'Neptune, the Mystic': we are far out in space, endlessly spinning. At the end of the piece, a women's choir sings a weird, disembodied chant as the suite fades to silence.

HOLST Gustav Holst (1874–1934) worked as an orchestral trombone-player, then as music teacher in a girls' school and an evening college. He was interested in English folk music and oriental mysticism, but, though both affect *The Planets*, it is mainly a show-piece, a demonstration of just what the symphony orchestra can achieve.

HOLST AND VAUGHAN WILLIAMS As students, Holst and Vaughan Williams made a promise that each would send the other every new composition, for comment and suggestion. Students often do this, but, unusually, Holst and VW kept it up for forty years, until the day Holst died. (You can often hear 'Holstisms' in Vaughan Williams, but apart from 'Jupiter', it's rare to hear the VW influence in Holst.)

NOW TRY Holst, *St Paul's* Suite (four delightful movements for his school string orchestra, ending with 'Greensleeves' set against a jig); ballet music, *The Perfect Fool* (like the 'Jupiter' and 'Uranus' movements of *The Planets*). Respighi, *The Pines of Rome*; Stravinsky, Suite from *The Firebird*.

IVES
The Unanswered Question

Ives lived in Connecticut, and often sat on his porch late into the night, star-gazing. He was fascinated by immensity, by the way the universe can seem to be a single vast entity, independent of humans and with thoughts and purposes we can never fully understand. He talked of a 'Universe' symphony, to be played by choirs and orchestras all over the countryside, each on a different mountain-top. Some of the music was to be by Ives, some by anyone else who wanted to contribute, and some by the players themselves as inspiration struck them. Even the rocks and clouds, he said, might be moved to join in.

The 'Universe' symphony was never more than talk. But this short piece gives some idea of the kind of music Ives had in mind. It is for three separate groups of players: a solo trumpet, four flutes and string orchestra. Each has independent music, and the conductor brings each group in whenever he or she feels like it. The strings play vast, slow-moving chords, seemingly without shape or purpose. The trumpet repeats a single phrase, like a nagging question. The flutes whistle and chatter aimlessly. Just as you think you've understood, it ends.

IVES   Charles Ives (1874–1954) studied music, but went into the insurance business and eventually became a millionaire. He composed in his spare time, never meaning his music to be performed, and wrote exactly as he pleased. A trumpet might 'visit' a piano sonata for a bar or two. Each performer in a piece might play in a different key and rhythm from everyone else. A few bars of 'Alexander's Ragtime Band' or 'Columbia, Gem of the Ocean' might feature in a symphony, or a hymn tune might become a fugue. When Ives's music was discovered and played after his death, people were amazed to find that instead of being the outpourings of a crazed eccentric it was meaningful, intriguing and often beautiful.

NOW TRY Ives, *Three Places in New England* (especially the stirring No. 2, 'Putnam's camp', and the beautiful river-piece No. 3, 'The Housantonic at Stockbridge'); 'Holidays' Symphony (especially the third movement, 'The Fourth of July'). Copland, *Quiet City*. Koechlin, *Les Bandarlog*.

JANÁČEK
Sinfonietta

This piece began when Janáček was asked to write fanfares for an athletics meeting: trumpet-calls echoing from side to side across the stadium. He was so pleased with the effect that he put the fanfares (and the twelve trumpets that play them) into a five-movement piece. They start it and end it, and in between times fragments keep bursting out of the other music, as if the excitement can hardly be contained.

The rest of the music also consists of fragments. Many are snatches of folk songs, or folk-song-like tunes by Janáček himself. They might last for ten seconds, or for as long as a minute. They are not so much composed as assembled into movements, like pieces of a particularly brightly-coloured jigsaw. All this sounds as if the Sinfonietta is a mishmash by a madman – but Janáček's ear-grabbing tunes (especially the fanfares) and his bizarre, unique orchestral sound carry all before them.

JANÁČEK   Leoš Janáček (1854–1928) ran a music school
for most of his life, and was a talented but not noticeably
outstanding composer until he was in his mid-sixties. Then,
unexpectedly, he fell headlong in love with a young married
woman. They never had an affair, but he wrote her over 600
impassioned love-letters, as emotional as an adolescent, and
hurled himself into vigorous composition. The two dozen
works composed during his seventies are original, fresh-
sounding and delightful: young man's music. It was almost
as if he lived his entire life backwards.

EXPLORING JANÁČEK   Janáček's biggest works are
operas: *Jenůfa* (stark tragedy), *The Cunning Little Vixen* (a
folk story performed by animals), *The Makropoulos Affair*
(surrealism: about someone who lives for centuries), and so
on. He also wrote songs, many choral works and a handful of
extraordinary, late chamber pieces including a Concertino
for piano and five instruments and two emotion-laden
string quartets (try *Intimate Letters*, love declarations for
string quartet, a jigsaw piece like the Sinfonietta but deeply
serious).

NOW TRY   Janáček, *Taras Bulba* (heroic rhapsody for
orchestra); *Mládí* ('Youth', a charming wind sextet based on
folk tunes, written when he was seventy); Glagolitic Mass
(the same jigsaw technique, and dazzling bright colours,
applied to a huge mass for choir and orchestra). Hindemith,
Concert Music for Strings and Brass. Bartók, *Dance*
Suite.

KHACHATURIAN
Adagio from *Spartacus*

In a competition for the silliest ballet story ever written, *Spartacus* would be hard to beat. Its hero is the gladiator who led a slave revolt in ancient Rome, and Khachaturian (a devout Stalinist) built into it a political message denouncing capitalism and applauding the heroic struggle of the workers.

However, in the midst of the daftness – gladiators and Roman legionaries battling each other in tights – is embedded a musical jewel. The ballet's sub-plot concerns the love between Spartacus and his wife Phrygia, and they dance several tender *pas de deux* which lift the score. The best, and best-known, is this Adagio, which consists of a simple tune repeated with ever-richer harmony and orchestration until it throbs and soars in an ecstasy of passion.

The work's odd history doesn't end here. In the 1970s, this Adagio was used as the signature tune for a TV series about nineteenth-century sailing ships (*The Onedin Line*), and it became an enormous hit. It has nothing to do with clipper ships, bellying sails and flying spume, but it fits them no better and no worse than it does the gladiators, and whatever its hidden meanings, it stirs the heart.

KHACHATURIAN Aram Khachaturian (1903–78) was Armenian, and his music has more than a dash of his native folk music, to Western ears some of the most exotic in the entire USSR. He wrote large-scale symphonies, concertos and sonatas, as any dutiful Soviet composer should, but their gorgeous tunes and peacock-tail scoring guaranteed them a popularity belying their names.

GAYANE If *Spartacus* is silly, Khachaturian's other ballet, *Gayane*, is even worse. Gayane is the wife of a treacherous collective farm owner. He plots to burn down the farm and cheat the workers, but is thwarted by heroic Kazakov, who is in love with Gayane. Having used this plot to pay his debt to the state censors, Khachaturian then thumbed his nose at them by writing not sober, politically correct music but a suite of Armenian folk dances. The 'Sabre-dance' was a huge hit in its day, and it, not to mention the various suites made from the rest of the ballet, are well worth tracking down.

NOW TRY Khachaturian, *Dance* Suite; Piano Concerto. Borodin, *Polovtsian Dances*. Enescu, Romanian Rhapsody No. 1.

KODÁLY
Háry János Suite

This suite uses movements from Kodály's farcical folk tale opera, and tells the same story. János is the village boaster. He spins a tale of how Napoleon's wife fell in love with him and took him to Paris – whereupon Napoleon, puce with jealousy, declared war on Austria, and János was forced to take up arms and defeat the French army single-handed.

The opera, and the suite, use Hungarian folk songs and folk dances, and the sound is led by the cimbalom (a piano-like instrument laid flat on a table and played with sticks held in the hands). The suite begins with an enormous sneeze – a sure sign, in Hungarian folk tales, that every word that follows is gospel truth. Six movements follow: 'The Fairy Tale Begins' (Háry gathers his audience in the village inn), 'Viennese Musical Clock' (for which the orchestra turns itself into a huge musical box), 'Song' (throbbing love music), 'The Battle and Defeat of Napoleon' (spoof fight music, and a sobbing funeral march led by saxophones), 'Intermezzo' (folk dance) and 'Entrance of the Emperor and his Court' (grand ceremonial finale).

KODÁLY Zoltán Kodály (1882–1967) was a friend of Bartók's and a fellow folk music collector. He became a leading educationist, teaching at the Liszt Academy in Budapest and devising a music-teaching system which is still used throughout Eastern Europe. From the 1920s onwards, he was also one of Hungary's most respected nationalist composers. During the Second World War, he helped many Hungarian artists to escape Nazi persecution, avoiding the concentration camps himself only because he was too well known and revered to be arrested. His music is even more saturated with folk music than is Bartók's, and it is tuneful, accessible and deeply felt. Often, a composer seems to sum up and symbolize everything that 'makes' his or her country, everything it holds most dear: Grieg in Norway, Tchaikovsky in Russia, Dvořák in Slovakia, Vaughan Williams in England. In Hungary, that composer was Kodály.

EXPLORING KODÁLY From Kodály's shorter works we recommend the orchestral *Dances of Marosszek* and *Summer Evening*, and the choral *Hungarian Folk Songs*. From his longer works, try the scintillating Concerto for Orchestra and the deeply moving choral cantata *Psalmus Hungaricus*.

NOW TRY Kodály, *Dances of Galánta*; 'The Peacock' Variations. Bartók, Concerto for Orchestra. Prokofiev, *Lieutenant Kijé*.

LEONCAVALLO
'On with the Motley' from *Pagliacci*

This aria, from Leoncavallo's opera *Pagliacci* ('Players'), originated one of the great twentieth-century showbiz clichés: the broken-hearted clown, forced to entertain even when crushed by personal misery. Canio, leader of a band of strolling players, is about to go on-stage as the cuckold Pulcinella, when he's told that his wife (who also plays his wife in the play) is cuckolding him for real. He sings this aria, then goes on-stage – and after an agonizing scene demanding to know the name of her lover (in the play, and, of course, for real) he stabs her and then kills himself.

An everyday story of theatre folk, perhaps (Leoncavallo did in fact base it on a newspaper report), but his sobbing, lacerating music takes us to the heart of the emotional experience as sure-footedly as any film score. The aria ('motley' is slang for stage make-up) was a sure-fire hit from the very first performance, and it was made famous worldwide in the 1900s when Caruso performed it on one of the first ever million-selling gramophone records.

LEONCAVALLO Ruggiero Leoncavallo (1857–1919) wrote half a dozen operas (including a *Bohème* that was outclassed by Puccini's, and an *Oedipus Rex* outclassed by Stravinsky's). *Pagliacci* was his one big success. It is short, and is usually performed in a double bill with Mascagni's equally melodramatic *Cavalleria rusticana*.

HOLD THE FRONT PAGE! *Pagliacci* may have been Leoncavallo's only success, but it made him a fortune, so that he had no need ever to work again. He devoted his time to good food, fine wine, and visiting performances of

Pagliacci in opera houses throughout the world. In one small Italian town theatre, the stranger he was sitting next to suddenly began gushing about the magnificence of the music. 'Nonsense,' snapped Leoncavallo. 'It's rubbish. That bit's stolen from Bizet; that part's lifted from Puccini; that section's appalling ...' Next morning, the local paper had front-page headlines: 'What Leoncavallo thinks of his own masterpiece'. For the town's theatre critic, a scoop; for Leoncavallo, the most embarrassing moment of his life.

NOW TRY Leoncavallo, Prologue to *Pagliacci* (similarly big, heart-on-sleeve aria, this time not for tenor but for baritone). Mascagni, 'Easter Hymn' from *Cavalleria rusticana*; Puccini, 'E lucevan le stelle' from *Tosca*.

LISZT
La Campanella

In the late 1820s, when Liszt was starting his career, the virtuoso violinist Paganini was the despair of the musical world. No one had ever played as he did; his technique and showmanship were so stunning that it was said that he'd sold his soul to the Devil. He wrote a set of Twenty-four Caprices for solo violin, and proclaimed that they were so formidable that no one could play them but himself – which was largely true.

No up-and-coming virtuoso could resist such a challenge. Liszt arranged several of the harder Caprices as *Transcendental Studies* for piano, making them ten times more difficult, and then put it about that only he could play them. *La Campanella* ('The Bell Tower') is one of them. Normally, we might expect a virtuoso show-piece to be clattery and triumphant. This is exactly the opposite. It never rises above a whisper, and it seems little more than a pretty tune played against a constantly repeated note, with a halo of sound round it like bells echoing across a valley. It's only when you see someone playing it that you realize that every muscle and sinew of the hands is being tested to the limit. 'Less means more', the professional's motto.

LISZT THE VIRTUOSO   Franz Liszt (1811–86) began his concert career at fourteen, and was soon swooned over like a prototype pop star. No other pianist could touch him; he was a friend (and lover) of princesses, and his romantic playing, devilish good looks and witty remarks made hearts flutter throughout Europe.

A spectator at an 1835 Liszt concert wrote afterwards: 'As the closing strains began, I saw Liszt's countenance assume that agony of expression, mingled with radiant smiles of joy, which I never saw in any other human face, except in the paintings of our Saviour by some of the early masters. His hands rushed over the keys, the floor on which I sat shook like a wire, and the whole audience was wrapped in sound ... Later, as I handed Mme de Circourt to her carriage, we both trembled like poplar leaves, and I tremble scarcely less as I write.'

NOW TRY Liszt, *Les Jeux d'eau à la Villa d'Este*; *Liebestraume* No. 3; *Mephisto Waltz* No. 1 (barnstorming). Chopin, *Berceuse* (gentle); *Souvenir de Paganini* (wild).

LISZT
Piano Concerto No. 1

Liszt was reluctant to share the stage with orchestras. When he did, he liked to steal their thunder — by, for example, following their playing of Berlioz's *Symphonie fantastique* with his own solo version, outdoing their effects. It was not until he retired from touring that he wrote his first concerto, in which soloist and orchestra compete on equal terms.

The concerto has showy moments – the piano's first entry, for example, sounds as if six people are playing, not one – but it is generally thoughtful rather than melodramatic. Its themes – abrupt, tender, virtuosic – wind in and out like dream-shapes. Those that stick in the mind are the gruff opening, a rustic flute tune (re-decorated by the pianist on each reappearance), a fleet-footed dance whose scoring made one critic complain that this was 'a concerto for triangle', and a yearning, slow melody eventually transformed into a march with showers of piano fireworks.

LISZT AND THE ORCHESTRA   In 1847, after giving up touring, Liszt was made conductor of the Weimar Court Orchestra, and threw himself into orchestral composition. He devised a new kind of piece, the 'symphonic poem', in which musical form was determined by story or mood. He invented new kinds of harmony and scoring. In short, just as he'd revolutionized piano playing, now he upturned people's views of what orchestral music could be like.

THE BEAR AND THE PUSSY-CAT   Liszt was often invited to parties, and always asked to play. One tactless hostess even dragged the piano into the middle of the room before he arrived, and when he did he searched in mock despair before asking, 'Don't you have a piano?' 'There in front of you, maestro.' 'Oh, good,' he said. 'I need somewhere to put my hat.' On another occasion, a young pianist advertised herself for a forthcoming recital as 'Pupil of Liszt', and was horrified to hear that he was visiting the town on the day of her performance. She ran to his hotel to beg forgiveness. He asked her to play, gave her some tips on pedalling, and said, 'Now you are a pupil. Best wishes. for tonight.'

NOW TRY Liszt, Piano Concerto No. 2. Saint-Saëns, Piano Concerto No. 2; Khachaturian, Piano Concerto.

LOLLIPOPS

CHABRIER, *Joyeuse marche*
No solemn square-bashing here; just a rollicking tune and irreverent high spirits. It's a bit brisk to march to, anyway.

CHOPIN, 'Revolutionary' Study, Op. 10, No. 12
In this the pianist's right hand plays a heroic tune, as abrupt as a challenge, while the left hand growls and thunders up and down the keyboard.

COPLAND, *Fanfare for the Common Man*
Famous as a theme of the Olympics, this is a sonorous thud of drums and an echoing, bell-like theme on wind and brass.

DUKAS, *The Sorcerer's Apprentice*
An apprentice told to fill buckets from a well steals a spell to make brooms do the work – and can't stop them. Mickey Mouse played the part in *Fantasia*, but with music as colourful as this who needs pictures?

ELGAR, *Pomp and Circumstance* March No. 1
As 'Land of Hope and Glory', this features at the Last Night of the Proms each year. But forget the words and the jingoism: it's a damn good tune.

FALLA, 'Ritual Fire Dance'
Flames leap and crackle as dancers imitate spirits in the shadows.

MOZART, *Eine Kleine Nachtmusik*
'A little serenade', written as muzak for a party. What muzak! Four delectable movements, instantly recognizable and still, every time, as fresh as paint.

MUSORGSKY, 'Song of the Flea'
The Devil sings this in Goethe's *Faust*. 'A flea, ha-haha-haha, a flea!' Over-the-top, but once heard never forgotten.

OFFENBACH, Barcarolle from *Tales of Hoffmann*
Seductive, swaying tune, imitating the rocking of a gondola in Venice. Health warning: once you hear it, you may not be able to get it out of your head for days.

PONCHIELLI, 'Dance of the Hours' from *La Gioconda*
This comes from one of the few operas ever written about Mona Lisa. 'Diddle-DIDDLE, diddle-DIDDLE ...' it goes, and ends with a breathless gallop. Time starts slowly, but then it flies ...

PUCCINI, 'Vissi d'arte'
In this aria from *Tosca*, the soprano sings one of Puccini's most long-drawn-out, full-hearted melodies, one glorious sound following another, as if time itself stood still.

RIMSKY-KORSAKOV, *The Flight of the Bumblebee*
A virtuoso violin piece, now usually arranged for wind-players, who love it because it lets them appear to play for two minutes on end without a breath. A stunt, but a good one.

SATIE, *Gymnopédie* No. 1

This is an extremely slow, sad waltz over a dragging accompaniment. Its tune is wispy but unforgettable. The enigmatic Greek title means 'Nude boy athletics'.

SINDING, *Rustle of Spring*

We all play the piano like this in our dreams: a soaring tune in one hand and swirls and eddies of accompaniment in the other – and then they swap.

VAUGHAN WILLIAMS, *Suite on English Folk Songs*

Good tunes and rum-te-tum accompaniments. This work is best on wind orchestra (as originally written), but is arranged for every conceivable combination. We couldn't choose between it and Vaughan Williams's *Fantasia on Greensleeves*, so we're recommending both.

VERDI, 'La donna è mobile'

Hit tenor aria from *Rigoletto*. The words are hardly politically correct – 'Women are fickle, drifting like thistledown' – and the tune swaggers and struts in suitably macho style.

MAHLER
Adagietto

This piece, the slow movement of Mahler's Symphony No. 5, became world-famous as the theme music for the film *Death in Venice*, about a dying musician obsessed by a beautiful boy. Scored for string orchestra and harp, the music builds from a scatter of single notes at the start (like slowly dripping water), first to a coherent tune, then to an edifice of huge, piled chords, before fading again to silence. Its pace never varies, and its mood is sustained throughout. Miraculously, it combines melancholy with heart-easing beauty, so that you are finally uplifted, not depressed.

MAHLER   Gustav Mahler (1860–1911) was the leading Viennese opera conductor of his day. In his spare time, on summer holidays by the Austrian lakes, he composed, chiefly songs and a series of ten massive symphonies. Apart from Nos. 1 and 4 (which are only fifty minutes long), each fills an entire concert, covering an enormous range of emotions, stretching the orchestra to the limit and offering the audience an all-engulfing musical experience. Mahler said that a symphony 'should contain the world', and for his legions of fans that's exactly what his own huge works achieve.

MAHLER THE CONDUCTOR   Mahler was a terrifying figure as a conductor. Tall, gaunt, with piercing eyes and an eagle's beak of a nose, he used the baton sparingly, directing the orchestra by glances, flicks of the wrist – and sudden, abrupt gleams and glints of rage or approval. In rehearsal, he was a martinet. If a note was marked *ppp*, then *ppp* it had to be. Failure to comply evoked a storm of sarcasm, and things had to be done to his satisfaction even if it took all afternoon.

DES KNABEN WUNDERHORN   'The Boy's Magic Horn' was a collection of folk poetry made in the 1800s, a verse parallel to Grimm's *Folk and Fairy Tales*. Mahler loved the poems' freshness and emotional directness, and made dozens of settings. Sometimes these are single songs, sometimes in groups (for example the charming *Lieder eines Fahrenden Gesellen* for voice and orchestra) – and sometimes they are inserted in symphonies (for example Nos. 1, 3 and 4), to magical effect.

NOW TRY Mahler, *Kindertotenlieder* (for voice and orchestra); 'Adagio' (first movement of Symphony No. 10). Barber, *Adagio for Strings*. Bruckner, Symphony No. 9. Górecki, Symphony No. 3.

MASSENET
'Méditation' (from *Thaïs*)

This rapturous piece, from a now-forgotten opera, is one of those numbers everyone recognizes but few can identify. It is played by all kinds of instruments – trombone, organ, electric guitar – but works best as Massenet wrote it, for violin and orchestra.

The 'Meditation' begins with a ripple of notes on the harp, against a background of shimmering strings. Over this, the violin sings a long melody which swoops and soars like birdsong. (This is one reason why the piece is never sung: it ranges too high and too low for any normal human voice.) The tune seems to go on for ever, as if the composer were endlessly threading beads of melody on to a necklace. The violinist has a short rest in the middle, but soon picks up the melody again, as if it were too precious to surrender, and carries it to an ecstatic, rapturous conclusion.

The whole thing is a triumph of sentimentality, and like most sentimentality, it has to be played absolutely from the heart to make its effect. Sent up, the 'Meditation' is rubbish; played properly, it can make you weep.

MASSENET   Jules Massenet (1842–1912) was professor of composition at the Paris Conservatoire, and a popular composer of songs, operas and oratorios. He wrote easygoing works with well-crafted star roles, and was a musical equivalent of such best-selling nineteenth-century novelists as Zola in France or Trollope in Britain. His biggest successes were *Manon Lescaut* in the 1880s (which is still in the repertoire) and *Don Quixote*, written thirty years later for the superb bass Chaliapin and (remarkably for an opera) made into a silent film.

WHOOPS! Massenet was a witty party guest. Once, after he'd spent the whole evening praising a fellow-composer, Reyer, his hostess said, 'How generous you are! Reyer's always so rude about you.' 'Alas, madame,' said Massenet, 'we're both such liars.'

OTHER MASSENET WORKS As a respite from vocal music, Massenet wrote suites of light music, fresh, unfussy and delightful. He called them holiday postcards in sound, and they have appropriate titles: *Neapolitan Scenes*, *Hungarian Scenes*, *Alsatian Scenes* and *Scènes pittoresques* ('Picturesque Scenes').

NOW TRY Massenet, ballet music from *Le Cid*. Elgar, *Chanson de matin*. Wolf-Ferrari, Intermezzo from *The Jewels of the Madonna*. Bruch, Violin Concerto No. 1 (slow movement).

MENDELSSOHN
Overture to *A Midsummer Night's Dream*

Mendelssohn, knocked sideways by Shakespeare's comedy, wrote this piece when he was just seventeen. The play has several strands: two pairs of lovers who stray into an enchanted wood, the squabbling king and queen of the

fairies, the ceremonial Athenian court, and a group of rustic
buffoons (led by Bottom the Weaver) rehearsing a play they
hope will win them fame and fortune. Mendelssohn
characterizes each group with music. The fairies are
represented by gossamer shimmering on high violins. The
court is shown by an expansive, flag-fluttering tune
interspersed with fanfares. A tangle of angry counterpoint
symbolizes the lovers, and the rustics are depicted by a
lumpish tune, breaking into ee-aws as the fairy king gives
Bottom an ass's head. The overture is good-humoured, witty
and exactly right for its subject: an achievement at any age,
and a miracle at seventeen.

A MIDSUMMER NIGHT'S DREAM   Seventeen years after
writing the overture, Mendelssohn wrote thirteen more
pieces of incidental music for a production of Shakespeare's
play in Potsdam, and, amazingly, they recapture all his
youthful freshness and sparkle. The suite involves a chorus
and solo singers ('You spotted snakes' is gorgeous), but three
movements for orchestra only are especially beloved: the
gossamer Scherzo, the Nocturne (with its glorious big tune
for horns), and the most-played Wedding March in Western
civilization.

MENDELSSOHN   Felix Mendelssohn(-Bartholdy) (1809–
47) was gifted at languages, mathematics, painting, writing,
and above all music. By the time he was seventeen he had
composed a hundred works, and after leaving university he
followed three musical careers: as virtuoso pianist, conductor (see page 115) and composer, achieving international
success in all of them. His first name (meaning 'Blessed')
could hardly have been better chosen.

MENDELSSOHN COMPOSING Mendelssohn's memory was phenomenal. He worked out his compositions to the last detail, in his head, before he wrote them down. A friend once visited him for a chat, but found him writing music. 'It's all right, I'm only copying,' Mendelssohn said. They talked for an hour before the friend realized that Mendelssohn had no document to copy from. He was holding an animated conversation, all the while 'copying' music which existed only inside his head.

NOW TRY Mendelssohn, *Hebrides* Overture. Schubert, *Rosamunde* Overture. Nicolai, Overture to *The Merry Wives of Windsor*.

MENDELSSOHN
Symphony No. 4, 'Italian'

Mendelssohn wrote this symphony in a fortnight, dazed with delight after his first visit to Italy. The piece begins with a sunburst of woodwind energy, accompanying a leaping violin tune – Mendelssohn said it represented the exaltation Italy produced in him. The second movement is a sound-picture of pilgrims processing along one of those dusty, cypress-fringed ancient Roman roads: a solemn melody over a trudging bass. The third movement, evoking a summer day in the countryside, is a relaxed rustic dance, filled with 'magic' horn-calls like those in *A Midsummer Night's Dream*. The last movement is a saltarello, a dance notable (on the dance floor) for the men's high kicks and the women's swirling skirts, and (in the orchestra) for the bubble of notes which underlies the tunes.

MENDELSSOHN AND THE SYMPHONY   In Beethoven's time, a generation before Mendelssohn, musicians had become used to the idea of the symphony as a grand, heroic endeavour, one of the greatest intellectual challenges a composer could undertake. Mendelssohn took a different line. His symphonies are lightweight and genial, entertaining rather than demanding. Two of them, the 'Italian' and the 'Scottish', are filled with memories of places he loved; another, the 'Reformation', does the same for Bach, 'visiting' his music and mulling over aspects of his style like someone relaxing over an album of remembered pleasures.

MENDELSSOHN ABROAD   Like many rich young people of his time, Mendelssohn spent the year after finishing university on the 'Grand Tour', visiting the cultural treasures and natural sights of Europe. He was overwhelmed, and for the rest of his life he hurried abroad on concert tours and holidays as often as he could. He found two countries particularly irresistible: Italy and Britain. In Italy, he tended to relax. In Britain, he combined hard work (playing for Queen Victoria, who idolized him, and conducting concerts all over the country) and 'relaxation' such as climbing mountains and tramping the coasts of Ireland, Scotland and the Western Isles. These visits fuelled his imagination, and some of his best-loved works – the 'Italian' and 'Scottish' symphonies, the 'Hebrides' overture, innumerable gondola pieces, Neapolitan songs and tarantellas for piano solo – grew out of them.

NOW TRY   Mendelssohn, *Hebrides* Overture. Symphony No. 3, 'Scottish'. Schubert, Symphony No. 3. Bizet, Symphony.

MENDELSSOHN
Violin Concerto

Mendelssohn wrote this work for his friend Ferdinand David, leader of the Leipzig Gewandhaus Orchestra, which Mendelssohn conducted. By all accounts, David produced a particularly sweet, pure tone on high notes, like someone whistling, and the concerto makes full use of that. Though not short of violin fireworks (David advised on the writing), the concerto is more relaxed, less heroic, than most: like a civilized conversation between old friends.

The first movement begins with one of David's special high, bright tunes, ending in scampering runs and decorations. A gentler, less hectic melody follows, and the rest of the movement makes play of the contrast, balancing show against reflection. (Show tends to win – this is, after all, a concerto. Particularly impressive is the cadenza, where the soloist seems at times to be doing an impression of someone trying to saw the violin in half.)

A long bassoon note leads to the second movement, a song for solo violin over murmured accompaniment. Another brief link takes us to the last movement, which is an irrepressible dance, setting fizzes of high notes from the soloist against chuckles and burbles from the woodwind. The end is ushered in when the soloists starts two minutes of athletic sawing, the orchestra keeps trying to interrupt, and they finally come together on a triumphant, long-held last note.

MENDELSSOHN AT LEIPZIG Mendelssohn was the first ever professional conductor. Until his time, the composer or orchestra leader directed the players and kept them together. Mendelssohn introduced the idea that the conductor should train the players, guiding them and moulding his or her own interpretation of the music. He made the Leipzig Gewandhaus Orchestra into one of the leading bands in Europe. (It still survives, as the longest-established orchestra in the world.) He revolutionized the repertoire, throwing out what he considered rubbish and introducing 'classic' works by Mozart, Beethoven and Handel. (One of these was Bach's *St Matthew Passion*, which was performed for the first time in a century.). He also negotiated proper salaries and pensions for the players, and broke with the old habit of interrupting symphonies and concertos to insert popular songs and novelty items, thus beginning the tradition of the orchestral concert as we know it today.

NOW TRY   Mendelssohn, Piano Concerto No. 1; Symphony No. 3, 'Scottish'. Bruch, Violin Concerto No. 1. Saint-Saëns, Violin Concerto No. 2.

MESSIAEN
Turangalîla-Symphony

On some temples in India, every square centimetre of wall-surface is covered with erotic carvings: people and animals coupling in every conceivable position, a monument to the exuberance and ecstasy of sex.

If one can have a sound-equivalent of these carvings, *Turangalîla* is it. It is a two-hour, ten-movement symphony for outsize orchestra, a sensual orgy. It creates its own world, and you can only succumb to it or reject it outright.

The Indian connection is vital. In Sanskrit, *turanga* means 'the rhythm of time' and *lîla* means 'play of the universe: birth, love and death'. That, no less, is Messiaen's theme. He mixes his sound-cocktail from the rhythms of Indian music and ancient Greek poetry, from birdsong, jazz, Roman Catholic chant, fanfares, church bells and cathedral organs, and blends it with solo piano, symphony orchestra, Far Eastern percussion instruments, and (literally above all) the disembodied, banshee squeal of the *ondes Martenot*, a 1930s electronic instrument to which he was addicted.

The symphony's ten movements alternate gush and jam session, and at their heart is a ten-minute explosion of sexual energy and rampant sound, one of the most orgasmic sequences ever put on paper. Messiaen called this movement, the fifth, 'Joy in the Blood of the Stars', and said that it represented the 'peak of carnal passion'. For newcomers to the work, it makes a superb taster for the whole experience.

MESSIAEN   Olivier Messiaen (1908–92) was the son of the mystical poet Cécile Sauvage, and he inherited her taste for extravagant exoticism. He was a devout Catholic, and the Mass and its music are at the heart of his inspiration. He also collected birdsong, notating the cries of over a thousand species and arranging them for instruments in many of his scores. (*Réveil des oiseaux* is made from nothing else.) He studied Greek and Sanskrit literature, Balinese music, Japanese religious opera, Indian classical music and jazz. From each, he took what he wanted, and they all colour his unique style. His works have extravagant titles – *Forgotten Offerings*, *From the Canyons to the Stars*, *Timecolour* – and the titles are matched each time by the sounds themselves.

NOW TRY   Messiaen, *Quatuor pour la fin du temps*; *Réveil des oiseaux* ('Dawn Chorus'). Tippett, Symphony No. 3. Ginastera, *Panambi*.

MOZART
Piano Concerto No. 21 in C major, K467

This concerto leapt to popularity in the 1970s, when its slow movement was used for the film *Elvira Madigan*.

Elvira Madigan is about the ecstasies and torments of young love, and the music of Mozart's slow movement seems to fit exactly. Muted strings set up a throbbing accompaniment, over which violins, then piano, play a long-breathed, rapturous melody. Mozart gives it a rhythmic 'kick' which adds even greater pathos. The accompaniment is mainly in groups of three notes, and he 'kicks' this by setting piano groups of two against them, a tiny confusion which first snags the mind and is then satisfyingly resolved as the rhythms come together again. Halfway through the movement the piano takes over the throbbing as well as the tune, woodwind join in with sighing, broken phrases, and strings pluck a rock-steady, march-like bass.

Although the slow movement stands well on its own, Mozart intended it as the centre-piece of a musical triptych, and the flanking movements add to its effect and are enriched by it. The first movement is martial – its opening anticipates the march beat underlying the slow movement – and is filled with spectacular runs and a big cadenza from the soloist. In the last movement a comic-song-like melody keeps alternating with more serious sections, until the final piano cadenza and the rush and tumble to reach the final chord.

MOZART'S PIANO CONCERTOS When Mozart was twenty-five, he resigned from a secure if unsatisfying job providing music to the Archbishop of Salzburg, and began a

precarious freelance existence. He earned his living from
teaching, opera commissions — and by giving public
concerts. For these, he wrote a series of piano concertos
(Nos. 15–27), and played them to enormous adulation. They
are miracles of tunefulness, wit and subtlety, among the
most enjoyable works he wrote — and there's nothing to
choose between them (at least for quality), so that if you like
one, you should like them all.

'K' NUMBERS   Instead of the Op. numbers attached to
most composers' works (short for *Opus*, 'Work'), Mozart's
have K numbers. These refer to the chronological catalogue
published in 1862 by Ludwig von Köchel.

NOW TRY   Mozart, Piano Concerto No. 23 in A major,
K488. Beethoven, Piano Concerto No. 1. Schumann, Piano
Concerto.

MOZART
'Voi che sapete' from *The Marriage of Figaro*

One complication in the plot of the *The Marriage of Figaro*
is the randy page-boy Cherubino. Having just discovered
sex, he's eager to investigate, and 'Voi che sapete' is the aria
in which he announces his feelings. 'Ladies, you know what
love is — tell me, is that what I have in my heart?'

The music begins as a decorous melody, suitable for a
page-boy who knows his place, then suddenly starts soaring
and leaping out of control. The accompaniment is breathless
and urgent, the harmony of the middle section in a bizarre
new key, as if Cherubino has suddenly stumbled into
unknown territory. The whole thing combines lilting

beauty with an eroticism which belies its formal, eighteenth-century good manners.

THE MARRIAGE OF FIGARO Today is Figaro's wedding day. But his employer, Count Almaviva, wants to seduce the bride-to-be – and the Countess is not pleased. The farce is completed by splendid minor characters – Cherubino, Don Basilio the music-teacher, Marcellina the housekeeper (who has her sights on Figaro), Antonio the gardener – and throughout, there is the ticking bomb of Figaro's true identity, to be revealed before the day is out.

MOZART Wolfgang Amadeus Mozart (1756–91) was a child prodigy, touring the courts of Europe from the age of eight. By fifteen he competed with adults on their own terms, and at twenty-five he was a freelance musician, earning a living from teaching, concerts and commissions for operas such as this one. He died at thirty-five, some say from a kidney disease aggravated by overwork, others from poison administered by his supposed rival Salieri.

EXPLORING MOZART From Mozart's shorter works, we recommend the sparkling Overture to *The Marriage of Figaro*, the 'Turkish Rondo' from Piano Sonata No. 8, K310, and the popular *Eine Kleine Nachtmusik* and Horn Concerto No. 4. From his more serious works, we recommend the concert aria 'Bella mia fiamma', the magnificent Sonata for Two Pianos, the Clarinet Concerto and one of his most sublime works in any form, Serenade No. 10, for 13 Wind Instruments, K361.

NOW TRY Mozart, 'Non so piú' (Cherubino's other aria); Catalogue Aria (from *Don Giovanni*). Rossini, 'Una voce poco fa' (from *The Barber of Seville*). Verdi, 'Reverenza' (from *Falstaff*).

MOZART
Symphony No. 40 in G minor, K550

The form of this symphony is as elegant and precise as a computer circuit-board. It is a perfect example of how to organize an eighteenth-century symphony, and its formal precision – its rightness – is a main part of its appeal.

There is, however, more. The surface of the music may be elegant, but the underlying emotion is dark and tragic. A Romantic composer (Berlioz, say) would have made these themes, these harmonies, burst passionately out of the orchestra, as if expressing suffering beyond endurance. Paradoxically, because Mozart corsets them with dainty, exquisite musical forms, their power is redoubled.

The symphony has four movements. From the opening bars the first is restless and questioning. Each positive statement (a sunny tune, for example) is undercut by a harmonic slither or an abrupt, loud chord. The slow movement is an unflustered melody decorated with distracted little wisps and flicks of harmony, and with a pulsing beat (mainly on horns) which adds menace. The third movement sandwiches two playings of a knotty, racked minuet round a middle section of radiant sweetness, the sunniest bars in the whole symphony. The finale picks up the urgent, unsettled mood of the first movement, so that the symphony, characteristically, comes to a neat full circle. It's not so much that form and emotional content make a triumphant match (this is not assertive music), but that Mozart leaves us feeling that we've made an emotional journey as we listened, that what we've heard has changed us.

MOZART'S LAST SYMPHONIES Most of the Mozart symphonies were written (often in short order, a matter of three or four days) for particular concerts or occasions. The last three are different. He composed them over a period of six weeks (quite a long time for him), and took extraordinary care over them. Yet they were not written for a concert, and he never heard them performed. They make a kind of trilogy: exuberant (No. 39), tragic (No. 40), triumphant (No. 41, 'Jupiter'). For anyone new to his orchestral music, they are a superb starting-point; for people who know his works, they remain among the peaks.

NOW TRY Mozart, Overture to *Don Giovanni*; Symphony No. 39. Haydn, Symphony No. 95. Schubert, Symphony No. 5.

MOZART
Oboe Quartet

Mozart wrote this quartet for himself and three friends, and gives them no quarter. Although the work is chamber music rather than orchestral, it is as taxing as any concerto. The players are equals (with the oboe, as it were, head of the family), and every note can be heard with total clarity, leaving no room for sloppiness, no hiding place.

The first movement is chirpy and extrovert. The main theme imitates someone whistling, and Mozart treats it sometimes with mock seriousness (making a fugue from it, for example), and sometimes decorates it with inconsequential spirals and whirls of scales. As soon as one idea is established the music scampers off in another direction, and the movement is over almost as soon as it begins.

The slow movement is a mock-tragic oboe aria over sobbing string chords – a doll's lament. The main tune of the finale is urbane and relaxed, and Mozart alternates it with episodes in different styles: teasing (the instruments tossing scraps of each other's phrases back and forth like ping-pong balls), mock-sad, and, as the work nears its end, a whirl of virtuosity as the oboist reminds us just who's boss.

MUSIC FOR FRIENDS Mozart had a childish, even infantile, sense of humour, and practising chamber music with him was an unpredictable pastime. While rehearsing this quartet, for example (he played the viola), he suddenly jumped up, cartwheeled round the room and started mewing like a cat (a dig at his oboist friend?). On other occasions he might put the music upside down, jumble up the parts or upset the music stands, leaving everyone to scrabble. For one particularly tolerant friend, he wrote a horn quintet in which the soloist's part was marked 'slow' when everyone else's was 'as fast as possible'. After his death one of his friends remarked, somewhat sourly, that his years as a child prodigy had made him 'all his childhood a grown man and all his manhood a little child'. Others, knowing the solemnity of most classical musicians, might think he was making a different sort of point.

NOW TRY Mozart, 'Skittle-alley' Trio for clarinet, viola and piano, K498 (so-called because Mozart was supposed to have scribbled it down during a game of skittles). Krommer, Wind Octet Op. 78. Schubert, 'Trout' Quintet.

MOZART
Requiem

Mozart's last work begins with a solemn prayer that the spirits of the dead may rest in peace. The mood is set by basset horns (tenor clarinets, among Mozart's favourite instruments), pleading against blaring brass chords, like foretastes of the Last Trump. The next movement depicts the Day of Judgement, complete with panic-stricken choruses, ominous trombone fanfares and foreboding from the tenor and bass soloists. Only the soprano and alto soloists lighten the mood, offering visions of redemption and heaven like sunshafts irradiating the darkness.

In the work's second half, despair is softened by the hope that God will remember the promise he made to Abraham. Thanks to Christ's mercy, our enemies will be scattered and we will take our places in Heaven with the righteous. The Requiem ends with a full-throated assertion of this idea. Earlier, the choral fugues sounded confused and terrified; now they are confident and trusting, as if humanity were not scattered but united in a single, radiant hope.

MYSTERIOUS STRANGER   In the play and film *Amadeus*, a hooded stranger visits Mozart and asks him to write this *Requiem*. Mozart superstitiously takes him for a visitor from beyond the grave, and assumes that the *Requiem* is to be for his own funeral. Soon afterwards, poisoned by Salieri, he dies. It's a good story, but the mysterious stranger is the only true thing in it. He came not from the Devil but from Count Walsegg, a nobleman who commissioned works from composers, anonymously, and passed them off as his own. The supernatural story was put about after Mozart's death, perhaps by his widow as a way of arousing interest in the

Requiem itself – and, stunt or not, it worked. The *Requiem* has been Mozart's most popular choral work ever since, and the story has an honoured place in musical (not to mention cinematic) myth.

SÜSSMAYR When Mozart died, the *Requiem* was only three-quarters finished. Anxious to earn money from it as soon as possible, his widow asked one of his pupils, Franz Xaver Süssmayr, to complete it. He did this so skilfully and discreetly that scholars are still squabbling about which sections were supplied by him and which written by the maestro.

NOW TRY Mozart, 'Coronation' Mass K317. Stravinsky, Symphony of Psalms (twentieth-century harmonies, but a similar mood).

MUSORGSKY
A Night On Bare Mountain

It is said in certain parts of Eastern Europe, that at mightnight on St John's Eve (the night before Midsummer Day), witches gather for an orgy whose master of ceremonies is Satan himself. Ordinary people who get mixed up in the celebrations become trapped in fairy time, so that what seems to them like a night's wild dancing is in fact a lifetime, and they end up withered and gibbering.

This is the subject of Musorgsky's barbaric orchestral piece. He gave it all the trappings of a witches' sabbath: frantic dances, gleeful woodwind shrieks, juddering rhythms and pounding drums. He also provided a programme – 'subterranean noise of spirits; apparitions, led by Satan; Satan-worship; black mass; witches' sabbath;

church bells heralding dawn; dispersal of spirits; daybreak'
– and depicted each item in high-gloss orchestral sound.

MUSORGSKY AND RIMSKY-KORSAKOV Musorgsky
planned *A Night on Bare Mountain* for an opera, *Sorochinsky
Fair*. But he never finished the opera, and only sketches of
Bare Mountain were found among his papers after his death.
His friend Rimsky-Korsakov set to work to assemble and
build on Musorgsky's ideas, and the result became a
favourite show-piece. Sixty years later, Musorgsky's original
score turned up, and proved even more outrageous and
extraordinary. This version, if available, is by far the best.
Orchestras still, however, programme Rimsky's revision –
hardly surprising, since it's less awkward to play, with
brilliantine sound rather than Musorgsky's spiky-haired
original.

MUSORGSKY Modeste Musorgsky (1839–81) lived a
tormented life, chiefly self-induced. From the age of twelve
he trained to be a soldier and at seventeen became an 'officer
and a gentleman' in a famous old regiment. Unfortunately,
heavy drinking was a regimental tradition, and by nineteen
he was an alcoholic. When he was twenty-five, his
aristocratic family was bankrupted overnight, and he was
forced to take a job as a clerk. The blow fuelled his addiction
and his neurotic disposition. He was a talented composer,
regularly beginning works of outstanding originality, but
he found it hard to match inspiration with concentrated
hard work. All we have of his music, therefore, is a handful
of finished pieces and a shelf of fragments, the rags of
genius.

Now try Musorgsky, 'Song of the Flea' (sung by the Devil in Goethe's *Faust*). Saint-Saëns, *Danse macabre*. Arnold, *Tam O'Shanter* Overture.

MUSORGSKY
Pictures at an Exhibition

The plan of this work is so simple it's amazing no one thought of it before. Musorgsky imagines himself walking round a picture exhibition, and each piece describes a painting. The pictures, by Victor Hartmann, survive: scenes from ordinary life and Russian folklore, brightly coloured and full of bizarre, surrealist touches – two aspects which Musorgsky's music exactly duplicates.

The ten 'pictures' are linked by a Promenade: a tune depicting the composer walking round the exhibition. This changes from picture to picture, as each painting affects his mood. The pictures are 'The Gnome' (angry), 'The Old Castle' (melancholy), 'Tuileries' (bustling), 'Bydlo' (rumbling: an old farm cart), 'Unhatched Chicks' (scampering), 'Samuel Goldenberg and Schmuyle' (conversation between two people, one assertive, the other cringing), 'Market-place at Limoges' (squabbling stall-holders), 'Catacombs' (sombre), 'Baba-yaga: the Hut on Fowl's Legs' (evoking the witch from a fairy tale) and 'The Great Gate of Kiev' (religious procession, complete with the pealing of innumerable bells).

MUSORGSKY AND RAVEL Musorgsky wrote *Pictures at an Exhibition* as a piano show-piece, and it is still often performed that way. But conductors felt that its variety and colour needed the full orchestra, and several arrangements have been made. The best known is by Ravel, and his scoring is so brilliant that it's hard to imagine that he didn't compose the piece in the first place. The moaning saxophone in 'The Old Castle', whining trumpet in 'Goldenberg and Schmuyle', and strings-and-woodwind carillon in 'The Great Gate of Kiev' (not a bell in sight) have to be heard to be believed.

MUSORGSKY'S TALENT Even when Musorgsky was drunk, he had musical class. Once, he was booked to accompany a singer he'd never met. His friends spent the whole day trying to sober him up — and then, in the dressing-room, he discovered the drinks cupboard. He had to be helped to the piano stool. It happened that the singer thought the keys of the songs too high, and wanted them played, at sight, a tone-and-a-half lower: a difficult feat at the best of times, never mind when drunk. Musorgsky performed so well that the audience suspected nothing, and the singer later said he'd never had such a sympathetic accompanist.

NOW TRY Musorgsky, *Night on the Bare Mountain*. Stravinsky, *The Firebird* Suite. Holst, *The Planets*.

NIELSEN
Overture to *Maskarade*

Maskarade is a breathless farce, and this overture superbly sets the mood. Horns and cellos set up a sonorous undercurrent, and the other instruments — piccolos, violins, trumpets, clarinets — scamper in with scraps of tune, runs and twirls, as eager as puppies. Towards the end everyone gets down to a final scurry, starting quietly and building, faster and faster, until a blare of brass and a final triumphant chord bring the curtain up and the fun can begin.

MASKARADE   *Maskarade* is Nielsen's setting of an irresistible comedy by Ludvig Holberg. In Copenhagen at Carnival time, two young people rebel (quite separately) against their parents, who want them to marry complete strangers. They change clothes with their servants, and send the servants (in carnival masks) to the formal entertainments, while they disguise themselves as servants and go, masked, for a fun-filled evening in the city. They meet and fall head over heels in love, and it's not until the last act, when the masks are off, that they find that their new lovers are exactly the people their parents wanted them to marry in the first place.

NIELSEN   Carl Nielsen (1865–1931) joined the army as a boy bandsman, then graduated to studying at the Copenhagen Conservatoire. He wrote the usual kinds of large-scale works – symphonies, sonatas – but in an original way, with happy tunes, quirky harmony and orchestration which incorporated the sounds of the country-dance groups and marching bands of his boyhood. His music is relaxed and happy; he is the Dvořák of Scandinavia.

BANDSMAN NIELSEN   In his memoirs, Nielsen remembers being terrified of his army instructor, a tall, grim man with cropped white hair, a clipped moustache and a forbidding manner. His mother took the instructor a chicken, and things were easier for a month or two. Then she began thinking of a duck. 'Ridiculous,' said Father. 'Leave the boy to cope.' 'Secretly I agreed with him,' adds Nielsen. 'We only had three or four ducks, and I was hoping to get a wing or a leg myself one day.'

Now TRY Nielsen, 'Dance of the Cocks' (also from
Maskarade); *Serenata in vano*. Bernstein, Overture to *Candide*.
Smetana, Overture to *The Bartered Bride*. Kabalevsky,
Colas Breugnon Overture.

NIELSEN
Symphony No. 3, 'Espansiva'

Nielsen was an autobiographical composer, always describing his own moods and feelings, and each of his six
symphonies is personal and evocative in an individual way.
Symphony No. 5, for example, is full of turmoil, inspired by
the First World War; Symphony No. 2 is a set of mood
pieces describing the four temperaments: Choleric, Phleg-
matic, Melancholic, Sanguine.

The 'subject' of Symphony No. 3, 'The Expansive', is
happiness. When people talk of 'sunny' music, this is what
they mean. It explores every degree of happiness, from calm
after a storm to exhilaration, from relaxation in beautiful
surroundings to the radiance of hope. The first movement is
a huge waltz, taking a simple dance rhythm and making it
tempestuous. The second movement is a placid country
scene, in which the music seems to get more peaceful with
every bar. At the movement's end, two wordless solo voices
join the orchestra: one of the most rapturous moments in
twentieth-century music.

The third movement is a rustic dance, the composer
remembering – and transfiguring – the village polkas for
which he played fiddle as a boy. The last movement is based
on a full-throated, ceremonial 'big' tune, which gradually
takes over the whole orchestra: a tune so welcoming that it's
all you can do, even in the concert hall, not to stand up and
sing along.

NIELSEN'S COUNTRYSIDE In Nielsen's memoir, *My Childhood*, he describes a sun-soaked afternoon from his youth – an exact match for the rapt slow movement of this symphony. 'We boys decided to spend our lunch-time tickling fish in the nearby ponds and peat-pits. I draped one arm over the lip of a peat-pit, and I could feel the crumbly soil warm in the sun. Beetles and ladybirds rustled and buzzed all round me, clambering about in the dry grass or leaping into flight. It was as if everything in the world was singing, a line of sound that blurred into drowsiness whenever a bumblebee or some other large insect hurried past, or when the grasshoppers took a moment's rest. We lay on the ground like cornstalks at harvest, without thought, without purpose, drunk on Nature's cocktail of sound, smell, sun and heat.'

NOW TRY Nielsen, *Helios* Overture (describing sunrise over the Aegean Sea); Symphony No. 4. Dvořák, Symphony No. 6. Sibelius, Symphony No. 2.

OFFENBACH
Orpheus in the Underworld

Offenbach's funniest operettas send up the gods and heroes of Greek myth. Zeus, Odysseus, Aphrodite, Helen of Troy are done over as never before or since.

Orpheus in the Underworld tells of the legendary musician whose singing was so beautiful that even trees and rocks hurried to hear him. When his wife, Eurydice, died, he went to the Underworld and charmed its gods to give her back. In Offenbach's version, Orpheus is an out-at-elbows violin teacher, Eurydice is a flirt, the Underworld is peopled by buffoons, and the censor keeps stopping the performance to check that nothing improper is going on.

Offenbach's music numbers are often played separately, the best known being the Cancan, a dance which outraged respectable Paris but so delighted everyone else that it became the show-stopping finale at the *Folies Bergère* and the Moulin Rouge. Others range from the soulful serenade 'When I was King of the Boeotians' (a tear-jerking tenor aria) to a wild chase as the Parisian Keystone Cops invade the stage.

ARRANGEMENTS   Offenbach's overture is a pot-pourri of the operetta's best tunes, and he also arranged a suite. The best of other people's selections is *Gaieté Parisienne* by Manuel Rosenthal – Offenbach's best tunes, from this and other scores, made into a single, picture-postcard-Paris, high-jinks ballet. Offenbach's music was also used for the film musical *Moulin Rouge*, perhaps the most lavish and colourful of all evocations of Paris in the belle époque.

OFFENBACH   Jacques Offenbach (1819–80), born in Cologne, began his career as a professional cellist, but soon moved into showbiz. He was a dandy and wit who pretended never to take life seriously, though he still managed to run a theatre and make a fortune. He and his friends were famous for their duels of wit, and the tradition survived his death. A friend went to call on him, and when told by the servant 'Monsieur Offenbach, alas, is dead,' immediately retorted, 'If he ever finds out, he'll be furious' – an epitaph even 'O. de Cologne' (as Offenbach signed himself) could hardly have surpassed.

NOW TRY Offenbach, *La Belle Hélène* (spoofing Helen of Troy). Sondheim, *A Funny Thing Happened on the Way to the Forum* (sending up ancient Rome). Sullivan, *Pineapple Poll* (superb follow-up to *Gaieté Parisienne*, using Gilbert and Sullivan hit tunes).

OPERA

EARLY OPERA

Opera was born in Renaissance Italy, when people were eagerly rediscovering ancient Greek and Roman culture. Believing that song was the main form of expression in ancient Greek tragedy, composers devised operas to recapture that style. They also used stories from Greek myth, as the ancient dramatists had done.

The greatest Renaissance opera composer was Monteverdi. His *Orfeo* tells of Orpheus's descent to the Underworld to charm the Dead with his singing and bring back his wife Eurydice. *Ulysses' Return* is about Ulysses' home-coming after the Trojan War. *The Coronation of Poppaea* recounts some bloodthirsty (and in Monteverdi's hands hilarious) plotting and skulduggery in ancient Rome. (Try *Orfeo* first.)

By the eighteenth century, operas were all the rage. Lavish opera houses were built throughout Europe (many of which are still in use today), and spectacular effects of all kinds were devised: burning cities, earthquakes, dragons, magic transformations. Star singers vied with each other to win applause, often moving hit numbers from one opera to another to please their fans. Once, Handel rashly gave one singer a song on horseback, and the rest of the cast immediately refused to go on unless each of them could have one too.

Handel's operas show this kind of 'number' opera at its best. Many are still performed, and dozens of arias are independently known. (We recommend, as extracts, 'Where'ere You Walk', from *Semele*, 'Ombra mai fu', from *Xerxes* and 'O Ruddier Than the Cherry', from the short *Acis and Galatea*, and, as a complete opera, *Agrippina*).

GLUCK AND MOZART

In the course of the eighteenth century, composers gradually shook themselves free of singers' vanity. They still wrote show passages and big tunes, but they balanced song and spectacle to make each opera a single dramatic whole. Two leaders in this movement were Christoph Willibald von Gluck (1714–87) and Mozart. Gluck was famous for the way he packed emotion into what seeemed the most simple melody, as can be heard in two extracts from his *Orpheus and Eurydice*, the flute solo 'Dance of the Blessed Spirits' and the lament 'Che farò senz' Eurydice', sung by Orpheus when he finds Eurydice dead.

Mozart's two dozen operas include four of the best loved in the repertoire: *Don Giovanni, The Marriage of Figaro, Così fan tutte* and *The Magic Flute*. He wrote superb solos – try the Catalogue Aria and the duet 'Là ci darem la mano' from *Don Giovanni*, or the Queen of the Night's arias from *The Magic Flute*. But his greatest gift was for clothing character and action in music. The finale to Act 2 of *The Marriage of Figaro* is dizzying farce, and the pace and verve all come from the music. In *The Magic Flute* there is a duet for two shy lovers, Papageno and Papagena, and the music matches every stammer and every blush. The final scene of *Don Giovanni*, when a

statue comes to life and drags the Don to Hell, can freeze
the blood even on record, without stage spectacle, by
musical means alone.

OPERA SINCE MOZART

Some composers (Rossini, for one) continued to write
'number' operas in the nineteenth century. But most
composers continued the changes begun by Gluck and
Mozart. In Wagner, Verdi and Puccini, the music is
continuous. The orchestra is not merely the accompaniment to the singers, but adds its own dramatic points, as
if it were a character. Stories also changed. Except for
Wagner (who based his operas on Norse myth), most
composers preferred historical characters or people from
everyday contemporary life. Verdi wrote an opera (*Don
Carlos*) about Charles V of Spain; Puccini wrote one (*La
Bohème*) about starving artists in 1850s Paris.

This idea, known as verismo ('truth-to-life'), was
sometimes undercut by the luscious music given to the
lead singers. As samples, we recommend the Verdi,
Puccini and Leoncavallo operas mentioned in this book,
and Tchaikovsky's *Eugene Onegin*, a tale of doomed
love which many consider his finest work. (Good
extract: Tatyana's Letter Scene.)

In the twentieth century, most composers scaled opera
down, making it more intimate, less spectacular, and
less dependent on huge star voices. For a taste of
twentieth-century opera, we recommend Stravinsky's
Oedipus Rex (a 1920s attempt to 're-invent' Greek
tragedy), Janáček's *The Cunning Little Vixen* (a folk-
tale opera in which the main characters are animals),

Richard Strauss's Vienna-and-cream comedy *Der Rosenkavalier* and Britten's magical fairy-opera *A Midsummer Night's Dream.*

OTHER OPERAS   See pages 35, 75, 76, 79, 102, 119, 131, 147, 148, 161, 193, 200, 215, 220.

ORCHESTRAL MUSIC

For many music-lovers, nothing equals the sound of a big classical orchestra in full cry. The united virtuosity and concentration of so many people, and the astounding variety of effects composers create for them, make their performances unforgettable.

In abstract orchestral music – such as most concertos (see pages 52–5) and symphonies (see pages 202–5) – sound-organization appeals for its own intellectual and emotional sake. Other kinds of orchestral music are often written to evoke specific scenes or tell particular stories. This kind of 'programme music' is the subject of these pages.

SUITES

Suites have been popular as long as orchestras have existed. Indeed, in the early eighteenth century they were the main kind of orchestral music, equalled only by concertos. Suites of that time consisted of six or seven movements. First came an 'overture', consisting of a ceremonial first section followed by a fleet-footed fugue. After this came the 'suite' ('following') itself: a set of dance movements and slow airs. Minuets, gavottes and hornpipes were popular, and most suites ended with a jig. Many composers wrote suites: good samples are Handel's *Music for the Royal Fireworks* and Bach's

Suite No. 2 (the movement called 'Chit-chat', 'Badinerie', is especially toothsome.) Our main recommendation is, however, Telemann. This maestro of the suite wrote more than a thousand – and though we can't claim to have heard them all we've never yet found a dud. Good ones to start with are *Don Quixote* and *Hamburg Ebb and Flow*. (In some catalogues, Telemann's suites are confusingly called 'overtures'. This is unnecessary pedantry: there's no connection with the kind of overtures people wrote a century later.)

In later times, a few composers also wrote dance suites. (Two superb examples are Respighi's dainty *The Birds*, clothing eighteenth-century pieces in twentieth-century orchestral colour, and Tchaikovsky's Suite No. 3, as full-blooded as any of his symphonies.) But most composers created suites of a different kind. They took specific stories or actual scenes (countries or landscapes), and evoked them in a series of musical snapshots. Fauré's *Dolly* Suite and Bizet's *Jeux d'enfants* are evocations of childhood; Grofé's *Grand Canyon* Suite and the suites Villa-Lobos called *Bachianas brasileiras* (try No. 2, conjuring up the Amazon jungle and the chugging 'Little Train of the Caipera') are pictures of landscape; Piston's *The Incredible Flutist* and Holst's *The Planets* evoke, respectively, a circus and outer space.

A third kind of suite is based on incidental music for plays, ballets, films and other shows. Writing for stage and screen concentrates a composer's mind wonderfully: the effects have to be exact, immediate and memorable, and even when the music is worked up later into a concert suite, these qualities remain. Suites of this kind begin with the eighteenth-century composer Rameau, who made collections of the orchestral sections of his operas (we recommend *Les Indes galantes* and *Les Boréades*.) In later times, the range is from the sublime (Beethoven's incidental music to Goethe's *Egmont*) to the sublimely silly (Ibert's *Divertissement*, music for the farce *The Italian Straw Hat*). From stage-music suites we recommend Fauré's *Masques et bergamasques* (refined), Schubert's *Rosamunde* music (tuneful) and Vaughan Williams's *The Wasps* (rollicking). From films we suggest Bernstein's gritty, jazzy *On the Waterfront* and Prokofiev's *Lieutenant Kijé*, and from ballet try two of the most satisfying suites of all, Copland's *Billy the Kid* and Stravinsky's *Pulcinella*.

SYMPHONIC POEMS

These are musical interpretations of stories or pictures. Each is usually a single movement, organized like one movement of a symphony (hence the name). Many composers wrote symphonic poems (we recommend Saint-Saëns's *Danse macabre* and Liadov's *The Enchanted Lake*), but the field belongs to three men in particular. Smetana wrote six symphonic poems depicting *Má Vlast*, 'My Country' (see page 189). Several of Richard Strauss's symphonic poems are based on folk tales (try *Till Eulenspiegel*); others start from books (for example *Also sprach Zarathustra*, whose opening was used for the launching of the spaceship in the film *2001*, and has featured in space programmes ever since); others describe his own life (for example *Ein Heldenleben* and the jokily titled 'Domestic' Symphony. Sibelius's symphonic poems depict the grandeur of his native Finland (*Finlandia*; *Tapiola*) and its literature (*En Saga*, 'A Saga').

OTHER WORKS

There are hundreds of other orchestral works, hard to squeeze into any particular category. Good samples are Weber's *Invitation to the Dance* (a soulful cello solo leading to a waltz), Delius's pastoral *On Hearing the First Cuckoo in Spring* and Rimsky-Korsakov's *Capriccio espagnole*, ('Spanish Caprice'), the orchestral showpiece to end them all.

FOR MORE ORCHESTRAL MUSIC See pages 1, 2, 13, 16, 28, 31, 37, 38, 44, 55, 58, 61, 67, 70, 72, 81, 85, 96, 97, 108, 111, 125, 154, 155, 157, 163, 179, 181, 187, 188, 191, 194, 195, 199, 207, 211, 212, 221, 223, 226.

ORFF
Carmina Burana

This unique work is the only choral cantata in Latin ever to reach the top of the classical pops and stay there. It's been a hit for fifty years.

Carmina Burana means 'Songs of Beuern', and refers to a collection of medieval poetry found in a dusty cupboard in the German monastery of Benediktbeuern. When the poems were translated, they were found to be anything but dusty. They are songs about the good life (at least as imagined by monkish poets): a non-stop orgy of drink, gambling, horseplay and above all sex. The texts are as cheeky as seaside postcards, and Orff matches them in music that is brash, raucous, bouncy and irresistible.

There are twenty-five numbers (each lasting about two minutes) arranged in three groups, and surrounded by prologue and epilogue. The prologue describes the wheel of fate, endlessly trapping us – so we might as well make the most of life. The three sections tell us how that should be done. 'Spring' says how charming and innocent the world is, all twittering birds, decorous dances and flirting. 'In the Tavern', about gluttony, centres on an unearthly song sung by a roasted swan, the centre-piece of a banquet which quickly becomes an orgy.

The third section, 'Love Game', starts virginally enough with solo soprano and boys' choir – but then the fun starts. A girl flirts with dress pulled high, and the men make bets about what might happen next. The music grows more and more frantic, until it explodes in a pounding chorus of sexual energy, followed by an ecstatic high soprano solo, 'Oh wonderful'. Immediately comes the epilogue: a hymn of adoration to Blanziflor and Helena, the medieval Romeo and Juliet, and a repeat of the first chorus, reminding us that however we enjoy ourselves, we are still trapped on the wheel of fate.

ORFF Carl Orff (1895–1982) concentrated on stage works: *Carmina Burana* was originally a ballet. Many are serious – operas based on Greek tragedy, for example – but several are as colourful and orgiastic as *Carmina Burana*, providing end-of-pier entertainment for the concert hall.

NOW TRY Orff, *Catulli Carmina*. Britten, *Spring Symphony*. Puccini, Gloria from *Messa di Gloria* (giving the same raucous, fun-filled treatment to – horror of horrors – the Mass itself).

OVERTURES

As the name suggests, overtures 'open' theatre shows, setting the scene for operas or plays. Many are straightforward medleys of the show's best tunes; others rework them in a more organized way.

In the nineteenth century, theatre overtures began to be detached from their parent works and performed in concerts. Their popularity led composers to invent a new form, the 'concert overture'. This tells a story or explores a mood, and also 'opens' a concert with a few minutes of jollity or pathos before the serious business of concertos, suites and symphonies gets under way.

ROSSINI, Overture to *The Thieving Magpie*

This overture introduces one of Rossini's most sparkling comic operas. After a mock-serious introduction (which fools some British audiences into thinking it's the National Anthem), it serves up tune after tune, working up to a splendidly straight-faced climax before collapsing into giggles. Good follow-up: Rossini, Overture to *Il signor Bruschino*.

MENDELSSOHN, *Hebrides* Overture

Mendelssohn wrote this overture (also known as *Fingal's Cave*) after visiting Scotland, and it's a sound-picture of the sea, calm at first, then lashed by a storm, then settling back to stillness. Good follow-up: MacCunn, *Land of the Mountain and the Flood*.

WALTON, *Portsmouth Point*

This jazzy overture was inspired by a picture showing the busy docks in eighteenth-century Portsmouth. Big chords keep silencing the bustle, as if some grandee were being carried through the crowd – and then hurry and scurry take over as if nothing had happened. Good follow-up: Vaughan Williams, *The Wasps*.

BERLIOZ, *King Lear*

This overture is not an introduction to the play, but is Berlioz's attempt to express the moods it inspired in him: tragedy, heroism and tenderness. Halfway through, he writes a savage orchestral storm, depicting Lear in his madness, defying the elements. Good follow-up: Brahms, *Tragic Overture*.

JOHANN STRAUSS, Overture to *Die Fledermaus*
Die Fledermaus is an operetta about love intrigues at a masked ball in nineteenth-century Vienna, and this overture showcases its biggest tunes. As Strauss is the composer, the tunes are chiefly waltzes and polkas, some of the most seductive he ever wrote. Good follow-up: Lehár, Overture to *The Merry Widow*.

FOR MORE OVERTURES   See pages 22, 28, 31, 41, 111, 128, 160, 206.

PAGANINI
Caprice in A minor

Paginini, the most phenomenal violinist of his time, intended his 24 Caprices to be the hardest music ever written for the instrument – so hard, in fact, that no one else would ever be able to play them. Hearing them is like watching a high-wire artist: death-defying stunts that keep your heart in your mouth, and your pleasure divided between expectation of disaster and delight when things go well.

This particular Caprice is a theme and variations, each more showy than the last. The idea caught other composers' attention, and soon everyone was writing variations on Paganini's theme. Over two hundred sets exist, ranging from Liszt's and Lutoslavski's virtuoso piano works to Andrew Lloyd Webber's Variations (theme tune of British TV's *South Bank Show*). If you had the stamina, you could fill your entire listening life with nothing else but variations on this theme – and the dance would be led by Paganini's own fiendish and intricate Caprice.

PAGANINI Nicolò Paganini (1782–1840) began his concert career at thirteen – and people were already so stunned by his talent that they claimed he'd been taught by the Devil himself. His wizardry survives in the pieces he wrote (including six concertos), which are still out of reach of all but the most flamboyant modern virtuosos.

PAGANINI AT WORK George Smart wrote of the extraordinary effect of Paganini's playing: 'Someone asked him to improvise on the violin the story of a son who kills his father, runs away, becomes a highwayman, falls in love with a girl who will not listen to him, leads her to a wild country spot and suddenly jumps with her from a rock into an abyss where they disappear for ever. Paganini listened quietly, and, when the story was at an end, asked that all the lights be extinguished. He then began playing, and so terrible was the musical interpretation of the idea that had been given to him that several ladies fainted and the salon, when relighted, looked like a battlefield.'

NOW TRY Paganini, Variations on 'The Carnival of Venice'; Violin Concerto No. 1. Sarasate, *Zigeunerweisen* ('Gypsy tunes'); Brahms, Variations on a Theme by Paganini (staggering piano virtuosity, one of the great keyboard show-pieces).

PROKOFIEV
Lieutenant Kijé Suite

Lieutenant Kijé ('Lieutenant Inkblot') started life as a comic film. The Tsar mistakes an inkblot on an official document for a real person's name, and takes an interest in the man's career. His officials are forced to invent a whole life history for Nobody: noble birth, love affair, super-gallant military career ... Unfortunately they do this so well that the Tsar summons Nobody for interview – and the officials are forced to contrive a glorious death in battle for their imaginary hero.

Prokofiev wrote witty music for this film, and later assembled the best movements into a suite. It tells the main episodes of Kijé's life. 'His Birth' is heralded by over-the-top fanfares and a march, announcing the heroic destiny to come. 'His Romance' is as tender and slushy as anyone could wish for (sweet nothings on tenor saxophone). 'His Marriage' is a ceremonial parade and a peal of bells. 'Troika' ('Sleigh-ride') is a Christmas-time journey through bracing cold, followed by a jolly tavern drinking song. 'His Death' is a desperately sad affair (saxophone again), interspersed with reminiscences of the highlights of his career.

PROKOFIEV   Sergei Prokofiev (1891–1953) specialized in two kinds of music. He wrote serious, sometimes grindingly discordant sonatas, symphonies and other large-scale concert works, and he put his sardonic sense of humour and ear for musical parody to work in some of the wittiest of all twentieth-century scores: *Peter and the Wolf*, Symphony No. 1, 'Classical' (spoofing Haydn), Piano Concerto No. 3 and two glittering ballets, *Romeo and Juliet* and *Cinderella*.

ROMEO AND JULIET Prokofiev set out to tell Shake-speare's story in straightforward ballet terms. Some of his music is romantic, influenced by such Tchaikovsky ballets as *Swan Lake* or *The Sleeping Beauty*, but he couldn't keep his tongue out of his cheek for long, and Shakespeare's pompous aristocrats and brawling gallants are given wonderfully spiky minuets, gavottes and other ancient dances – the formal world of the past seen through a distorting mirror, and enormous fun.

NOW TRY   Prokofiev, *The Love of Three Oranges* Suite; *Romeo and Juliet* Suites Nos. 1 and 2; Piano Sonata No. 9. Shostakovich, *The Age of Gold* Suite. Khachaturian, *The Comedians* Suite. Martinů, *La Revue de cuisine*.

PUCCINI
'Nessun Dorma' from *Turandot*

Every Puccini opera depends on at least one magnificent, show-piece tenor aria like this. The plot grinds to a halt, everyone stands back and the lead singer launches into a stream of honeyed sound. The aria ends, the enraptured audience demands an encore – and the opera starts up again as if nothing had happened.

'Nessun dorma' is a song of defiance. Princess Turandot has been told that if she can find out by morning the name of her mysterious suitor, he will die. None shall sleep: everyone in the kingdom must search for the name. The suitor, Prince X, sings this aria. 'None shall sleep, but none shall find my name. It's locked in my heart, and what my secret is, none shall ever know.'

Nothing stands in the tenor's way as he sings this tune. The accompaniment is plain, organ-like orchestral chords.

Violins accompany his tune, following every nuance, every slowing-down or speeding-up, every change between loud and soft. The voice floats on an air-cushion of sound, effortless, heroic and superbly sensual. We all know that there will be high notes, tenor notes to shake the building – and Puccini delays them right to the end. A theatrical magician is at work, and all we need to do is listen.

TURANDOT In ancient China, a cruel princess kills suitors who fail to answer three riddles. One day a mysterious prince arrives and answers all three, ending with the princess's own name (Turandot). She is distraught, and he generously says that she can have one more chance: if she guesses his name before dawn, she can kill him after all. She fails, but thanks to thinking about him all night, she's fallen in love with him.

PUCCINI Giacomo Puccini (1858–1924) trained as a church composer, but was seduced by theatre in his early twenties and never looked back. He wrote a dozen operas, among them such hits as La Bohème, Tosca, Madame Butterfly and Turandot, and specialized in melodramatic plots and that glorious, unfettered singing known as bel canto ('beautiful song') to millions of devotees.

NOW TRY Puccini, 'Che gelida manina' (La Bohème); 'O mio babbino caro' (Gianni Schicchi). Donizetti, 'Una furtiva lagrima' (L'Elisir d'amore). Verdi, 'Celeste Aida' (Aida).

PUCCINI
Madame Butterfly

The story of *Madame Butterfly* began as a novelette, then became a theatrical barnstormer in the USA, and finally conquered the world in Puccini's operatic version. It has everything: an exotic location (Japan), a beautiful, hapless heroine, a double-dyed villain, a tiny child and a tragic death.

B.F. Pinkerton (or as he was prudently renamed in early English versions of the story, 'F.B.' Pinkerton – standing, we're assured, for 'Francis Blummy'), a lieutenant in the US navy, marries beautiful Cho-cho-san ('Madame Butterfly') while on manoeuvres off Japan. He returns to the USA, and the plot moves on three years. We see Butterfly alone with her and Pinkerton's child. He has deserted her. She sings of how he will return ('One Fine Day'). A ship arrives – it's his! She prepares to welcome him, but he appears with another woman, his American wife. Cho-cho-san promises not to make trouble, if they will only bring up the child. Then she blindfolds the toddler, gives him an American flag to play with, goes behind a screen and kills herself.

Puccini uses real Japanese tunes in the music, not to mention 'The Star-Spangled Banner'. But the rest of the time he gives us his usual full-throated melodies and ecstatic harmony. Singing is what this opera is about, and in Puccini's hands the waif-wife Cho-cho-san becomes a magnificent dramatic soprano, and her music uplifts and overwhelms. It's a miracle that such a glorious weight of emotion and sensuality can be carried on such a flimsy story, but it's emotion and sensuality that make the opera unforgettable.

PUCCINI STORIES   Puccini was a celebrity, but he liked to play the game of being an ordinary man, with everyday pastimes. He claimed that his hobby was smoking – mentioning nothing of the fact that he used to sit and smoke in five-star hotel suites, while the staff fought off hosts of adoring fans. He went duck-hunting, with reporters and *paparazzi* splashing in the reeds behind him. He played cards, and whenever he was dummy he sat at the piano and worked at his latest masterpiece (usually winning the evening as well, thanks to the wearing effect this had on his opponents' nerves).

NOW TRY Puccini, *La Bohème*. Mascagni, *Cavalleria rusticana*. Verdi, *Aida*.

PURCELL
'Dido's Lament' from *Dido and Aeneas*

This aria comes at the end of the opera. Queen Dido of Carthage is in love with Prince Aeneas of Troy, who has been driven to her kingdom by storms. But the gods call him away to fulfil his destiny (of founding Rome), and he abandons her. Distraught, she sings this aria, and then kills herself.

Purcell loved the musical form of the chaconne, in which a bass tune is endlessly repeated without change, while different, ever-changing melodies and harmonies appear above it. 'Dido's Lament' follows this pattern. The bass line (played on its own at the beginning) is slow, dragging, despairing. Over it, the contralto soloist sings a melody which combines pathos and soul-rending beauty ('When I am Laid in Earth'). The melody has a refrain like a tolling bell: 'Remember me! Remember me!'

DIDO AND AENEAS   Purcell wrote this opera in 1689 for his friend Josiah Priest, who ran a girls' school in Chelsea. It may have been a money-raiser, performed by friends of the composer and headmaster. But some people think that it was written actually for the pupils, and that this explains its comparatively small scale and the large amount of soprano-heavy choral singing and dancing. Either way, *Dido and Aeneas* was one of the first full-scale operas written in English, and it caused a sensation.

PURCELL   Henry Purcell (1659–95) combined three careers. He was organist and choirmaster of Westminster Abbey; he was a favoured royal composer, writing music for great occasions and court entertainments, and a busy theatre writer, producing incidental music, operas, and a host of popular songs. His death, so the story goes, was caused by this last career. His wife resented the time he spent in theatres and in theatre pubs. She told the servants to lock the doors at midnight, and to let no one in afterwards. One wet night, Purcell came home in the small hours, was forced to wait outside all night – and caught a fatal chill.

NOW TRY   Purcell, *Music for Awhile*; *Evening Hymn*. Dowland, 'Flow, Flow My Tears'. Lawes, 'Sitting By the Streams'. Bach, 'Erbarme dich' ('Have Mercy, Lord'), from the *St Matthew Passion*.

RACHMANINOV
Prelude in C sharp minor, Op. 3 No. 2.

Rachmaninov wrote this piece when he was nineteen, and sold it to a publisher, outright, for a handful of roubles. He then introduced it at a piano recital, and it made a sensation.

Over the next few years it brought him worldwide fame. For the rest of his life, wherever he went and whatever else he played, audiences demanded it; when he was sixty-nine, with a shelf full of mature masterpieces to his name, he was still best known by a piece he'd written as a boy half a century before. If he'd kept the copyright, this one short piece would have made him a millionaire.

Rachmaninov may have come to hate his 'Frankenstein's monster' (as he once called it), but it's easy to see why audiences adored it. It has no story, but conjures up atmosphere and mood so decisively that by the end you feel as satisfied as if you'd heard an entire dramatic scene. It begins with hectoring bass notes accompanied by anguished chords higher up the keyboard. The lower the bass descends, the higher the chords climb, as if trying to escape. The middle section is a pleading melody accompanied by agitated runs and flutterings; then the dominating opening music returns to end the piece.

RACHMANINOV   Sergei Rachmaninov (1873–1943) was not only a composer, but one of the great piano virtuosos of the twentieth century. He settled in the USA at the time of the Russian Revolution, and never went home. Like many exiled creators, however, he filled his works with nostalgia for his native land; in fact he is one of the most 'Russian' of all composers. His works include symphonies, sonatas, operas, songs (little known, but worth seeking out), and some of the most popular piano music ever written.

EXPLORING RACHMANINOV   From his shorter works, we recommend 'Vocalise' (originally a song, but better known as an instrumental solo), the piano solo Prelude Op. 23 No. 5 and the beautiful Eighteenth Variation from *Rhapsody on a Theme of Paganini*. From his longer works,

try the whole of the *Rhapsody on a Theme of Paganini*, the
riply Romantic Symphony No. 2 and the bubbly Symphonic
Dances.

NOW TRY   Rachmaninov, Prelude Op. 32 No. 5; Prelude
Op. 23 No. 9. Chopin, 'Revolutionary' Study, Op. 10 No. 12;
Polonaise Op. 40 No. 1.

RACHMANINOV
Piano Concerto No. 2

In 1897 Rachmaninov's first symphony failed in the concert
hall, and he plunged into a four-year depression, convinced
that he would never work again. He was cured by a
psychiatrist who built up his confidence with hours of
patient praise and persuasion, and in 1901 he premiered this
concerto. It was one of his finest works, and became the
best-loved concerto in the entire piano repertoire.

Hollywood discovered the concerto in the 1930s, and
made it a star. In one musical, 200 dancing-girls play it, four
to each piano, and the pianos come to life and dance. In a
horror film, a dead pianist's hands are grafted on to the arms
of a murderer, and semiquavers alternate with strangling. In
one war movie, the finale's big tune is set to the words 'Full
Moon and Empty Arms' (sailors yearning for their dear
ones). In another, *Brief Encounter*, Celia Johnson falls in
love with Trevor Howard in a station waiting-room, while
this concerto breaks our hearts on the soundtrack.

The concerto starts with piano chords leading to a
sonorous string melody, accompanied by piano ripplings.
The music builds to a full-throated climax on the big main
tune. The slow movement is a delicate piano reverie over
orchestral murmurings. The last movement contrasts

martial bustle and the 'Full Moon' tune – and the battle, inevitably, is won by melody.

RACHMANINOV AND STRAVINSKY   It would be hard to imagine two composers less alike than romantic Rachmaninov and dry Stravinsky. They lived in Hollywood, but avoided one another. One day their wives, fed up with this interminable, unspoken quarrel, arranged a dinner party. After a somewhat edgy meal, R. and S. retired to the drawing room with a bottle of vodka. Tiptoeing in later, the wives found them maudlin. Stravinsky had discovered that Rachmaninov had sold his greatest hit, the C sharp minor prelude, outright, and Rachmaninov had found out that Stravinsky had done the same with the *Firebird* Suite. As the vodka level sank, the two musical giants had spent a happy time with paper and pencil working out just how rich they'd have been if they'd insisted on royalties.

NOW TRY Rachmaninov, *Rhapsody on a Theme of Paganini*; Piano Concerto No. 3. Grieg, Piano Concerto. Liszt, Piano Concerto No. 2.

RAVEL
Pavane pour une infante défunte

Ravel always said that he gave this piece its title, 'Pavane for a Dead Infanta', simply because he liked the sound of the words. He wrote it originally for piano, then arranged it for orchestra, and it made his name.

    For all Ravel's claims, the title does seem to have something to do with the music. In sixteenth-century Spain, at times of royal mourning, all entertainments were replaced by a kind of stately ceremonial – and that's the mood this music seems to catch. It consists of a sad melody, repeated many times over endlessly changing accompaniment. There is no progression, no feeling of climax: the piece begins, moves on and ends. We might be watching a procession, or looking at the frieze of some solemn royal funeral. Jewel-like melancholy, sadness precisely focused – these few short bars seem to hint at feelings far more complex than they describe.

RAVEL Maurice Ravel (1875–1937) had an amazingly acute ear for sound, and as a student he developed a new kind of harmony based on the overtones of bells – something few of his professors could understand. It served him all his life, and gives his music unique sound-quality. He wrote much for piano, but was also a superb orchestrator, so that many of his compositions exist both for piano and for orchestra, and fascinate the ear equally in either format.

PIANO OR ORCHESTRA Two Ravel scores to explore in both forms (piano solo and orchestra) are the suites *Ma mère l'oye* ('Mother Goose'), sound-pictures of such children's fairy stories as 'Tom Thumb' and 'Beauty and the Beast', and *Le tombeau de Couperin* ('Couperin's Memorial' – another title chosen mainly for its sound), four pieces blending eighteenth-century dance forms with spiky harmony and Basquish tunes. Each started life for piano, and was then so dazzlingly orchestrated that it's hard to imagine it written for anything else. Composition students are often told to study and compare both versions, and the result (something few other composers' works achieve) is to make you want to rush away and try similar experiments yourself.

Now try   Follow-ups to piano version: Ravel, *Sonatine*. Debussy *La Fille aux cheveux de lin*. To orchestral version: Ravel, *Ma mère l'oye*; Fauré, *Après un rêve* (instrumental version).

RAVEL
Boléro

Even experts need to practise, and Ravel spent years promising himself the luxury of trying some experiments in orchestration as soon as he had time. His chance came when the dancer Ida Rubinstein asked him to orchestrate some piano music by the Spanish composer Albéniz. Ravel couldn't get the rights, and offered instead to write Rubinstein an original piece in Spanish style.

Boléro was the result. It is in bolero rhythm; a slow, hypnotic beat, with a distinct 'thump-THUMP' emphasis at the end of each bar. Originally the dance was accompanied by strumming guitars and clacking castanets, both of which Ravel avoids in his orchestration. He wrote a single, 32-bar span of melody, which is played, in sequence and without change, over and over again throughout the piece, to the accompaniment of the insistent bolero rhythm. What gives variety is the scoring. Each 32-bar segment has new harmony and new instrumentation. The piece is organized as a continuously mounting climax – and when it reaches its peak, the key dramatically changes (for the first time in seventeen minutes), and the work ends with an orchestral slump and slither, as if exhausted.

Parallels between all this and the sex act were not lost on performers – from Ida Rubinstein to Dudley Moore (*Boléro* features in the seduction scenes in Blake Edwards' film *10*) and the ice-dancers Torvill and Dean. Sweet nothings, foreplay, union, orgasm – not a stage is ignored, so that what began as a study in orchestration becomes a hypnotic, and highly explicit, tour de force.

PIANO AND ORCHESTRA   Ravel wrote two piano concertos, and they are among his finest works. The first has jazzy outer movements, full of spiky Basque themes and some languorous Spanish harmony; these surround a delicate slow movement, traceries of piano notes which miraculously remind you of Mozart and Chopin at the same time. The second concerto, for left hand alone (though you'd never guess unless you saw it performed) is dark, sinister and mysterious, in a world of erotic mystery which Ravel often explored with relish.

NOW TRY   Ravel, *La Valse*; *Daphnis and Chloé*, Suite No. 1. Falla, 'Ritual Fire Dance'. Honegger, *Pacific 231*.

RESPIGHI
Fountains of Rome

This orchestral show-piece is as explicit as film music, though its pictures are entirely in the mind. Respighi obligingly provides a detailed programme. He took four fountains, and set out to 'express the feelings and visions they evoked, choosing for each the time of day when it was most in harmony with the surrounding landscape, or appeared most beautiful to the observer'.

The first movement, 'The Valle Julia Fountain', is a murmurous, pastoral piece, in which, Respighi said, 'cattle pass by and disappear in the fresh, damp mists of a Roman dawn'. The second, 'Triton Fountain in the Morning', is lively horseplay, sea-nymphs and sea-gods frolicking in a 'frenzied dance amid the water-jets'. The third, 'Trevi Fountain at Noon', is solemn and triumphal, representing 'Neptune's chariot drawn by sea-horses and leading a procession of sirens and tritons'. The fourth, 'Villa Medici Fountain at Sunset', is an evocation of evening: birds singing, bells tolling, leaves rustling, and all 'dying peacefully away into the silence of the night'. The whole work is played continuously, making a sound-picture of Rome from dawn to dusk.

RESPIGHI   Ottorino Respighi (1879–1936), amazingly for one of the master orchestrators of his time, was never sucked into writing for films. He spent his time composing and conducting operas (now largely unknown outside Italy), and suites for orchestra which offer sound-pictures as explicit as those in *Fountains of Rome*: *Botticelli Triptych*, *Stained-glass Windows*, *Impressions of Brazil*, *The Birds*, and the 'Roman Triptych' *Fountains of Rome*, *Pines of Rome* and *Roman Festivals*.

THE HIDDEN RESPIGHI   Unexpectedly, perhaps, for a man with such extrovert, hot-blooded ways with the orchestra, Respighi was also fascinated by medieval and Renaissance church music, particularly plainchant. He never wrote church works of this kind himself, but instead composed a dozen delicate, plain-as-a-glass-of-water instrumental pieces in ancient style. They tend to be eclipsed by his huge orchestral scores, but they are available on CD and are a restrained delight: *Concerto in the Old Style* and *Gregorian Concerto* for Violin and Orchestra, String Quartet, Violin Sonata, 'Doric' Quartet and the delightful cantata *La Primavera*, 'Spring', for soloists, choir and orchestra.

NOW TRY   Respighi, *Pines of Rome*. Ibert, *Escales* ('Ports of Call'). Villa-Lobos, *Bachiana brasileira* No. 2. Rimsky-Korsakov, *Capriccio espagnole*. After *La Primavera*: Nielsen, *Springtime on Fyn*.

RIMSKY-KORSAKOV
Sheherazade

After the death of Alexander Borodin in 1887, Rimsky-Korsakov helped to finish composing his *Prince Igor*. Delighted by the *Polovtsian Dances*, he planned an 'Oriental' work of his own, based on the Arabian Nights stories about Sindbad the Sailor. Rather than setting out to retell them in music, though, he preferred to give 'the general idea of a story of fairy-tale wonders', and the resulting piece is a 'symphonic' suite, organized like a symphony, not a set of unconnected movements.

The music centres on a solo violin tune, which represents Sheherazade spinning tales to woo her husband the Caliph. It reappears in each movement, binding the work together and creating its atmosphere of delicious, Oriental mystery.

The first movement, after Sheherazade's theme, is based on a slowly rocking idea, suggesting a ship butting its way through unknown seas. The second movement is a lively festival, and the third is swaying and sinuous (suggesting to some listeners the sweet nothings of lovers, and to others a belly-dance). The fourth movement returns to the idea of the ship, this time involved in a storm and a battle with a particularly savage giant.

DIAGHILEV AND *SHEHERAZADE*   In the 1900s, when Diaghilev was looking for exotic ballet subjects to showcase his star dancer Nijinsky, he fell on *Sheherazade*. A story was devised, full of genies, scimitars and supernatural monsters; choreography was prepared to show off Nijinsky's athletic leaps, bared chest and flashing teeth; sets were built as exotic as dreams – and success was assured. On the crest of the ballet's fame, Rimsky-Korsakov's music became a worldwide hit, and has been so ever since.

RIMSKY-KORSAKOV   We hear much about child prodigies, but Nikolai Rimsky-Korsakov (1844–1908) was something much rarer: an adult prodigy. Until he was thirty, he was a naval officer; then he taught himself counterpoint, harmony and orchestration, so successfully that he was appointed Professor at the St Petersburg Conservatory. His friends and pupils included some of the most distinguished Russian composers of the time (Borodin, Musorgsky, Tchaikovsky, Glazunov, Stravinsky), and he left a couple of dozen masterworks: operas, symphonies, choral pieces, and the barnstorming orchestral works which keep his name alive.

NOW TRY Rimsky-Korsakov, *Capriccio espagnol*; *Russian Easter Festival* Overture. Berlioz, *Roman Carnival* Overture. Respighi, *Pines of Rome*.

RODRIGO
Concierto de Aranjuez

Acoustic guitars are quiet instruments, and their accompaniments need to be subtle rather than assertive. Rodrigo uses an orchestra of a couple of dozen players, who rarely all play at once. The guitar is like the leader in chamber music, and the music is more agreement than confrontation.

As its name suggests, the concerto is saturated with the sounds of Southern Spain. Andalusia is the home of flamenco, and of that heartbroken, sobbing lament called *cante jondo*, 'deep song'. Rodrigo's music also reminds some listeners of another Andalusian idea: dressage. Teaching horses to dance, or at least step rhythmically to music, was carried from there throughout Europe (for example to the famous Spanish Riding School in Vienna).

Rodrigo's concerto begins with guitar strumming, as if the soloist were improvising. The orchestra takes up the theme, player after player, until it becomes the accompaniment to a straight-backed, prancing tune. Everyone has fun with this, until the movement, having said what it came to say, stops.

The slow movement (once top of the instrumental pops) is a *cante jondo*, a lament over strummed chords. It appears first on cor anglais (alto oboe), then on guitar, then on full orchestra. Each time, new decorations are added, so that by the end every single note has a trill or twist, like the breaks in someone's voice as they sob. The guitar ends with an anguished, thrumming cadenza, interrupted by the orchestra as if it can stand no more pain.

The finale is in complete contrast. It's in a jaunty, now-you-see-it-now-you-don't rhythm. The strings make playful counterpoint of the tune. The woodwind chirp. The guitar skitters and skips, until with a last headlong tumble from top to bottom, and two orchestral plonks, it's over.

RODRIGO   Until Joaquin Rodrigo (born 1902) was forty, composing was a hobby: the success of this piece made it possible for him to write music full-time. (At first no one would publish it – 'Who wants a guitar concerto?' – so he brought it out himself, and made a fortune.) He has written two dozen other concertos, for different instruments, all similarly light-hearted and imbued with Andalusian sun.

Now TRY Rodrigo, *Fantasia para un gentilhombre*; *Concierto pastorale* (for flute and orchestra). Castelnuovo-Tedesco, Guitar Concerto No. 1. Falla, Harpsichord Concerto.

ROSSINI
Overture to *William Tell*

William Tell is a zestful operatic mixture of historical drama and swashbuckling romance. The story is taken from real history – the heroic struggle of the Swiss, led by William Tell, against Austrian domination. But in Rossini's hands, Tell becomes a kind of Robin Hood, a legend in his own lifetime, and attention is paid to such picture-postcard aspects of Switzerland as brooding mountains, lush green meadows and Romantic storms.

All these things figure in the overture. Like many overtures of the time, it is partly a medley of songs from the opera. But Rossini also makes it a kind of tone poem, a sound-picture of Alpine scenery and derring-do which stirs our hearts even before the curtain rises. It opens with a slow theme for cellos alone, and this leads straight to a melodramatic, explosive storm. The sky clears, and a cor anglais (alto oboe) plays a pastoral melody, accompanied by chirps and tweets on solo flute. Trumpets sound, and the orchestra gets down to the main business of the overture: a gallop which grows ever more heroic and frenzied, and which has become so well known that the first half-dozen notes are enough to remind anyone in the Western world of high adventure, the heart-thudding, *Boys' Own Paper* gallantry of every ripping yarn there ever was.

ROSSINI   Gioacchino Rossini (1792–1868) wrote his first opera as a student, and by the time he was thirty he was the best-known composer in Europe. Until 1829 he produced at least two operas a year: comedies, dramas, epics, tragedies. Then, abruptly, aged thirty-eight, he retired. He spent the last thirty-eight years of his life enjoying his wealth, showing off to fans, consuming gargantuan, gourmet meals (Tournedos Rossini was invented for him) and resisting offers to take up his composing pen again.

ROSSINI OVERTURES   Each Rossini opera has its overture, and most have become even more famous than their operas. There could be no better introduction to his music – and few jollier openings to a concert – than the overtures to *The Barber of Seville*, *The Thieving Magpie*, *The Silken Ladder* or a dozen others.

NOW TRY   Rossini, Overture to *The Italian Girl in Algiers*. Weber, Overture to *Oberon*. Berlioz, *The Corsair* Overture. Suppé, Overture to *Light Cavalry*.

ROSSINI
The Barber of Seville

Count Almaviva wants to marry Rosina, but Rosina's guardian Dr Bartolo has other plans for her. Alamaviva pays Figaro, the town barber and 'fixer', to find ways of getting him into Bartolo's house to meet Rosina, and then to spirit her away and marry her. First Figaro disguises him as a drunken soldier looking for lodgings, then as a music teacher come to give Rosina a singing lesson – and when all else fails, he organizes a midnight elopement.

Rossini's music miraculously aids this headlong, feather-light farce. The opera is a soufflé of patter-songs, sentimental arias, serenades and ensembles in which everyone is singing the same music but is uttering completely different thoughts. Highlights include the overture, Rosina's aria 'Una voce poco fa', the 'Calunnia' aria ('Gossip spreads and grows enormous'), Figaro's famous 'Largo al factotum' ('Fee-ga-ro, Fee-ga-ro, Fee-ga-ro', much used in TV adverts), and the brilliantly funny finale to Act 2, involving a midnight elopement in a thunderstorm, hampered by a chorus of Keystone Cops police.

ROSSINI, MUSIC AND FOOD   'I can think of nothing better than eating,' Rossini once said. 'The heart has love, the stomach has appetite. It's like a conductor, leading the orchestra of our emotions and whipping it into action. The bassoon's grumbling and the piccolo's shrieks of longing remind me of an empty stomach. A full stomach's a satisfied triangle or a joyful kettledrum. The four acts of the comic opera of life are food, love, song and good digestion. They fizz like bubbles in a bottle of champagne – and if you let them pop without enjoying them, you're a fool.'

ROSSINI AND BEETHOVEN   Some highbrows turned up their noses at Rossini, just as 'serious' theatre-lovers still often sneer at farce. But not all of them. In 1822 Rossini went to visit Beethoven. The great man said, 'Rossini, eh? Composer of *The Barber of Seville*? That will be played as long as Italian opera lasts. Keep doing that.' Rossini expressed admiration of his genius. Beethoven said with a sigh, 'Oh, un infelice' ('I'm useless'). As he showed Rossini out, he repeated, 'Don't forget to write more *Barbers*.'

Now TRY Rossini, *Cinderella*; *The Italian Girl in Algiers*. Donizetti *L'Elisir d'amore*. Mozart, *The Marriage of Figaro* (written earlier, but a sequel to the events of this opera).

ROSSINI (arranged by RESPIGHI)
La boutique fantasque

Although Rossini wrote no operas in his 'retirement', he did compose songs, piano works and other short pieces. A visitor once found him scribbling diligently away, and asked what he was doing. 'It's my dog's birthday tomorrow, and I'm writing him something. I always do.' He called these pieces 'Sins of my old age', and refused to let anyone publish them.

The 'Sins' are sparkling, witty and as tuneful as anything from Rossini's 'working' years. In 1919 Diaghilev asked Respighi to arrange some of them as a ballet, retelling the children's story which Delibes had earlier used for *Coppélia*, about a toymaker's doll which magically comes to life. *La boutique fantasque* ('The Fantastic Toyshop') was the hit of the 1919 London season, and its music quickly became popular as an orchestral suite.

La boutique fantasque has eight short movements. A semi-solemn overture leads to a series of dances: tarantella, mazurka, cossack dance, cancan, slow waltz. The mood changes briefly for a sentimental nocturne, before a galop brings the work to a riotous conclusion. Many of the pieces are known in their own right – the ballet is pillaged for adverts – but nothing beats hearing them together, in Respighi's sumptuous orchestration, 'sins' turned out as blessings.

ROSSINI ONE-LINERS   Rossini's wit was famous, and he spared no one. Liszt once visited him, and improvised wildly. 'Thanks,' said Rossini, 'but I prefer the chaos that starts Haydn's *Creation*'. Asked what he thought of Wagner, he said, 'Wagner has wonderful moments – but terrible quarters-of-an-hour.' Baron Rothschild, maker of Château-Lafite, once sent him a bunch of grapes from his own private hothouse, and Rossini sent them back, on the grounds that he never drank wine in pill-form.

STRING SONATAS, WIND QUARTETS   After Rossini's death, not only 'sins of old age' were discovered. As a boy, he had written apprentice works, put them in a cupboard and forgotten them. They are unpretentious, fresh and charming: six string sonatas and six wind quartets. No sign of the opera composer to come – more like Mozart or Schubert with his hair down.

NOW TRY   Rossini, overtures to *La gazza ladra*, *Il Signor Bruschino*. Britten, *Matinées musicales* (also based on some of Rossini's 'sins'). Offenbach, arranged Rosenthal, *Gaieté parisienne*.

SAINT-SAËNS
Carnival of the Animals

Saint-Saëns wrote this 'grand zoological fantasy' for a Mardi Gras concert given by a cellist friend. The concert was an annual event, featuring musical jokes and spoofs of all kinds. (On another occasion, Chabrier composed for it a set of polkas and galops, based on the most serious, gut-wrenching themes from Wagner's *Ring of the Nibelungs*.)

Saint-Saëns's fantasy, for two pianos, flute, clarinet, xylophone and strings, is a grand procession of animals. After preliminary groanings and heavings, as if cages were being wrenched open, a quick flourish from the pianos and a pompous fanfare, the lion pads past, leading the march and roaring most satisfactorily. Hens bustle after him, brainlessly twittering and marshalled by a bossy cockerel. A herd of mules gallops past, followed by turtles, lumbering along to a slowed-down version of the galop from Offenbach's *Orpheus in the Underworld*. Next come kangaroos and an aquariumful of fish.

At this point, things get really silly. Donkeys bray, a cuckoo calls from the woods, an aviary of budgies answers, and the two pianists desperately start practising scales and arpeggios. Fossils dance (to a bony rattle from the xylophone), a swan sails serenely by – cello solo, the best-known movement of them all ('The Swan') – and then everyone takes their places for a final, demented dance built from every musical theme we've heard so far.

SAINT-SAËNS   By the time Camille Saint-Saëns (1835–1921) was five he was playing Beethoven sonatas; he played concertos at seven, and was a full-blown virtuoso at ten. (He used to practise scales each morning with the newspaper propped on the music stand.) He was a fine organist, a theatre composer (writing, among other things, a dozen operas), a conductor and a teacher. At the age of eighty-six, he was still working fourteen hours a day. His music is witty, tuneful, fun to play and unfailingly attractive.

EXPLORING SAINT-SAËNS   From his shorter works, we recommend the witches' sabbath *Danse macabre* for orchestra, the aria 'Softly Awakes My Heart' from his opera

Samson and Delilah) and the dazzlingly virtuosic *Introduction and Rondo Capriccioso* for violin and orchestra. From his longer works, we recommend Variations on a Theme of Beethoven for two pianos, the Cello Concerto No. 1 and the symphonic poem *Le Rouet d'Omphale*.

NOW TRY Saint-Saëns, *Wedding-cake Caprice*. Ibert, *Divertissement*. Britten, *Soirées musicales*.

SAINT-SAËNS
Symphony No. 3 (Organ Symphony)

Saint-Saëns played the organ part at this symphony's première in 1886, in a concert at which he also played Beethoven's Piano Concerto No. 4.

Saint-Saëns was concerned that some of the symphonies of the time – Brahms's, for example – were too massive, too grand, to be taken in at one hearing. It wasn't the fault of the ideas, he said, it was simply that there was too much 'meat' for the average listener to digest. Hence the scheme of this symphony. It's long (forty minutes plus), and has the standard four movements. But it's organized in two equal halves, each of which balances heavyweight sections against lighter, more delicate music. The whole symphony is also based on a single main theme throughout, so that every turn and twist of the musical argument is obvious, clearly derived from the same instantly recognizable idea.

The theme comes right at the start, after a brief introduction. It's like plainchant, very similar to the *Dies irae* chant famous since medieval times. To begin with, its mood is urgent and bustling, and Saint-Saëns contrasts it with gentler, more relaxed material; then, in typical fashion, both kinds of music are played together. Everyone then settles down to a slow, church-voluntary section, making use of the organ's most religious, most ethereal sounds. The second section begins by transforming the main theme into a spiky, fantastical Devil's dance, with huge brass chords and quicksilver piano runs glinting through the orchestral texture. A building-shaking organ chord stops this in its tracks, and the work ends with a massive fugue.

PIANO CONCERTO NO. 2   The best-loved of all Saint-Saëns's concertos balances a long first movement against two shorter ones, grouped as a pair. The first movement is anguished and serious, with heavyweight flourishes from the piano. Then, as if saying 'That's enough of that', Saint-Saëns sweeps it away with a gossamer scherzo (complete with galumphing middle section) and a fleet-footed tarantella. Piano concertos have never been so toothsome.

NOW TRY   After the symphony: Saint-Saëns, *Marche héroïque*; *Le Rouet d'Omphale*. Liszt, *Les Préludes*. d'Indy, *Symphony on a French Mountain Air*. Poulenc, Organ Concerto. After the concerto: Saint-Saëns, Piano Concerto No. 4. Franck, Symphonic Variations.

SCHOENBERG
Verklärte Nacht

Schoenberg originally wrote this piece for string sextet, but he later arranged it for string orchestra, and this is the version we recommend.

At the beginning of the twentieth century, the Expressionist movement was a feature of all the arts. As their name implies, the movement's exponents were interested in direct expression: no hints or ironies, but clear, blunt statements of emotion and feeling. Expressionism was particularly strong in painting, and one such picture, Munch's *The Scream* (showing a terrified woman rushing across a bridge towards us, looking as if transformed from human being into a single screaming mouth) has become one of our ragged century's most familiar images.

Schoenberg tried to put the same ideas into music, replacing older means of structure, harmony or melody with the straightforward depiction of emotion in sound. *Verklärte Nacht* ('Transfigured Night') tells a specific story. A man and woman walk through a shadowy, moonlit forest. She is tense and anxious; he is mystified. Suddenly she blurts out that she's had an affair and is pregnant. He forgives her, and they walk on, their love transforming the night.

Schoenberg gives a theme to each of the ideas in this story: moonlight, shadow, incomprehension, panic, forgiveness, love. If the work has shape, it comes from the contrast between the panic music of the start and the ecstatic music of the end. But the whole point is that is has no form: it is as fluid, suggestive and disturbing as a dream.

SCHOENBERG Arnold Schoenberg (1874–1951) developed his expressionist ideas by seeking to remove from music all the old emotional associations of keys and formal harmonies and trying to make each sound exactly equal to all the others. His later music can seem wild and chaotic at first, but after a few hearings it seeps into your mind, arousing responses at a level no other composer's music seems to touch.

BOILING SEA Schoenberg had devoted followers, and equally passionate detractors. He once said that his crusade was like 'swimming in a boiling sea', and when he was asked

why he'd taken up such a thorny musical path, he said
wryly, 'No one else was volunteering, so it was up to me.'

Now try Schoenberg, *Five Pieces for Orchestra*.
Richard Strauss, *Metamorphosen*. Berg, *Three Pieces for
Orchestra*.

SCHUBERT
Symphony No. 8, 'Unfinished'

Schubert wrote this symphony in 1822, but he put it aside
and never heard it. After his death one of his friends rescued
the manuscript, and the symphony was eventually played
thirty-seven years later.

No one knows why Schubert broke off composition, a
few bars into the third movement. Some think that he
sketched the whole symphony but lost the sketches or used
them in other works; or that he was offered better-paying
work and put the symphony aside. Others say that the two
surviving movements are so satisfying that he decided to
add no more. (This is the view of most audiences. The
symphony is a favourite concert piece, and no one seems
bothered by the fact that it's a musical equivalent of the
Parthenon ruins or the Venus de Milo.)

The first movement begins with an oboe solo over
anxious strings, followed by a glorious cello tune. The
orchestra plays with these two ideas, in particular the
contrast between bumpy rhythms and smooth-flowing
melody – and it keeps interrupting itself with loud, brassy
chords, as if the argument were too intense to continue. The
slow movement is another contrast: a tune in calm chords,
serene as heaven on some painted church ceiling, and an
angular middle section before the serenity returns.

SCHUBERT   Franz Schubert (1797–1828) began his career as a schoolteacher, but he was so bad a disciplinarian that he gave up. He then earned a precarious living as a composer of lightweight piano pieces and songs: at the time no publisher was interested in his major works. He composed from dawn to noon each day, feverishly starting one work as soon as the previous one was finished. He spent the rest of his time with friends, eating, drinking (for which he was famous), partying and making music. It was a hectic life, and burned him out (he died at thirty-one): it was almost as if he worked so frantically because he knew he had little time.

SCHUBERT AT WORK   Schubert's concentration was legendary. A friend once wrote: 'You call on him. He's working. He grunts, "Hello, how are you?" You go away.'

NOW TRY   Schubert, Symphony No. 5; String Quintet. Mendelssohn, Symphony No. 4. Bizet, Symphony in C.

SCHUBERT
Four Impromptus, D899

Schubert wrote piano music of every kind, from heavyweight sonatas to sets of waltzes (originally improvised for 'Schubertiads' – see page 171). The Impromptus come somewhere in the middle. They are easy enough for amateurs, but not beneath the dignity of virtuosos. They are solidly constructed, but unfailingly light-hearted and tuneful. Their name suggests that they, too, began as party improvisations, worked up later when Schubert wrote them down.

The Opus 90 set contains four pieces, usually played in sequence as a suite. The first is a march, full of pompous

strutting and assertive single notes like trumpet-calls. Next
come a fast, featherlight waltz and song-like slow tune over
one of Schubert's favourite rippling-water accompaniments. The fourth, best-known, impromptu begins with
showers of fast notes in the right hand over a dignified left-
hand tune, continues with a bombastic minor-key melody
over pounding chords, and then repeats the raindrops.

SCHUBERTIAD 'Schubertiad' was the name Schubert's
friends gave to evenings which began with food and drink,
went on with music (usually composed and played by
Schubert) and ended with dancing (for which Schubert also
often played). They were favourite entertainments, and
often there were three or four a week, lasting until well into
the small hours. In fact, Schubert himself usually left early,
before the fun ended; he had serious composing to do, as
soon as it was dawn.

FOUR HANDS, ONE PIANO Piano duets were a popular
nineteenth-century form of home music-making. Symphonies, string quartets, even operas were published in duet
arrangements – a good way for music-lovers to get to know
them in the days before recording. Schubert was one of the
few composers to write original works for duet, and these
range from light music, marches and variation-sets to full-
scale fantasies and sonatas. The first of his three *Marches
militaires* is one of his best-known short pieces, and his
Fantasy in F minor is a large, virtuoso composition,
stretching this most intimate of forms to its limit and highly
satisfying both to play and to listen to.

NOW TRY Schubert, Four Impromptus, Op. 142; *Moments musicaux*, Op. 94. Mendelssohn, *Songs Without
Words* (Book 5, Op. 62; including the famous 'Spring

Song'). Grieg, *Holberg Suite* (piano version). Mozart, Piano Duet Sonata in B flat K358.

SCHUBERT
Songs

Schubert wrote more than six hundred songs. A friend once said that 'he no sooner glanced at a verse of poetry than it became a song' – and there were stories of him scribbling songs on menus and table napkins, composing them in the time it took to write them down.

Few composers have ever rivalled Schubert's gift for matching a poem so exactly in music that the two can hardly be imagined separately. He seems to get underneath the surface of the words to express their inner meaning. In 'The Erlking', for example, about a father desperately galloping to save his sick child from the Devil, the hammering accompaniment suggests not just horse's hoofs but also the (unmentioned) terror and pounding of the father's heart. In 'Ganymede', about a beautiful boy snatched to Heaven to be the gods' cupbearer, the music gives a feeling of breathless anticipation; not something overtly expressed in the words, but exactly (one imagines) what anyone might feel if caught up in such an experience. In 'Who Is Sylvia?', the piano part balances an excited right-hand part and an expansive tune in the left hand, beautifully catching the mood of relaxed happiness which radiates from Shakespeare's words.

This idea, of giving the accompaniment a half-share in musical meaning with the voice, was common enough in opera, but rare in songs – until Schubert. He took it to apotheosis in a couple of large 'song cycles': groups of songs telling a single story and meant to be performed entire. In *Winterreise* ('Winter Journey') the words tell of despair, dead hopes and lost love – and the piano part seems frozen, all emotion iced. In *Die Schöne Müllerin* ('The Maid of the Mill'), the boy-meets-girl, boy-loses-girl story is accompanied by burbling piano throughout, representing the mill-stream which witnesses the young man's changing moods.

Now TRY It's hard to recommend specific Schubert songs, out of so many. As well as those mentioned above, famous names include 'The Trout', 'Gretchen at the Spinning Wheel', 'Heidenröslein' ('Hedge-rose') and 'To Music' – but they are no better than hundreds of others whose names are less familiar. Anthology recordings or recitals are probably the simplest way to sample the experience. Other outstanding song composers: Brahms, Grieg, Rachmaninov, Schumann, Wolf; we particularly recommend Wolf and Rachmaninov.

SCHUBERT
Octet in F major

From 1800 well into the 1820s the most popular classical music work in Vienna was Beethoven's Septet. It was played in concert halls, at private parties, in arrangements of all kinds, and its tunes were adapted for barrel-organ and played around the streets. Professionals and amateurs alike began looking for a sequel, and Schubert, asked to provide one for a rich clarinettist, leapt at the chance of emulating his idol Beethoven and making some cash at the same time.

Beethoven's Septet is scored for three wind instruments and string quartet. Schubert added a double-bass for extra sonority. But, like Beethoven, he remembered his patron, the clarinettist who commissioned the piece. In this Octet, though all players are equal, when it comes to big tunes or chances for display, one instrument is more 'equal' than all the others.

Schubert followed the ground-plan of Beethoven's Septet. There are six movements: the usual symphonic four, plus an extra minuet and a set of variations. His 'symphonic' movements are larger-scale than Beethoven's: serious rather than frivolous. The first movement follows a tragic introduction with an argument based on the contrast between an urgent, striving theme and a simple song tune with elaborate decorations by clarinet and first violin. The second movement is placid and slow, close in feeling to the 'By the brook' movement from Beethoven's 'Pastoral' Symphony. The third movement is an energetic scherzo and trio and the finale, after another tragic introduction, blends march and dance. The two inserted movements are the fourth, a variation-set which gives everyone a chance to shine, but especially the acrobatic first violin and the graceful clarinet. The fifth movement, minuet and trio, highlights solo horn.

'TROUT' QUINTET   Schubert's 'Trout' quintet, an exuberant piece he wrote to play with friends in 1819, features solo piano (originally Schubert himself), violin, viola, cello and double-bass. It's like a piano concerto in chamber music style. There are five movements, the usual symphonic four plus one, and this added movement gives the piece its nickname, since it's a set of variations on Schubert's cheerful song 'The Trout'.

NOW TRY   Schubert, 'Death and the Maiden' string quartet. Beethoven, Septet. Spohr, Nonet. Saint-Saëns, 'Military' Septet.

SCHUMANN
Träumerei

Träumerei ('Dreaming') is a musical equivalent of the
famous Victorian picture of a little girl with curly hair and a
beribboned dress sitting on a footstool gazing into the fire.
We never share the pictures she sees there: all we see is her
dreaminess, her reverie. A single phrase is played four times.
It begins in the same way each time, then wanders off in a
different direction before falling back and starting again.
Each time it comes the wandering is a little longer, a little
more purposeful – but still the piece ends (as reveries
should) quietly, sedately, inconclusively.

SCHUMANN   Robert Schumann (1810–56) trained to be a
concert pianist, but an injury to his hand forced him to
change careers. He became a critic and composer, writing
some of the most surging and eloquent of all romantic
music. He married Clara Wieck, one of the nineteenth
century's leading concert pianists, and they had a large
family. Unfortunately, family contentment was not
matched by private peace. All his life Schumann suffered
from depression, and in the 1850s it became so serious that
he attempted suicide, was committed to hospital, and died
insane.

SCHUMANN AND THE PIANO   Schumann used the piano
the way a painter uses a sketch-pad. He scribbled down
impressions of everything he saw and felt. No emotion,
reflection or memory was too fleeting to capture in sound.
He wrote dozens of piano suites, with titles like *Butterflies*,
Scenes from Childhood (*Träumerei* is No. 7 of this set),
Short Stories, *Forest Pictures* and *Album Leaves*. He

organized his suites intellectually, for example by repeating themes, or working ideas out from movement to movement – he was addicted to codes and 'secret' messages, such as building into the texture musical notes from his beloved's name. This means that each piece in a suite affects all the others and is affected by them; the suites gain if heard complete.

NOW TRY Schumann's piano suites make excellent follow-ups to each other. The rest of *Scenes from Childhood* (*Kinderscenen*) make a good starting-point, followed by *Butterflies* (*Papillons*) and *Carnaval*. Good follow-ups by others to *Träumerei* are Debussy, *Clair de lune*, Grieg, *To the Spring* (piano solo version) and MacDowell, *To a Wild Rose* (from *Ten Woodland Sketches*).

SCHUMANN
Piano Concerto

In most classical music involving orchestra, there is a strong feeling of intellectual control – a sense that the music has been organized and assembled in a way owing as much to the head as to the heart. (With such large forces, one might imagine, it could hardly be otherwise.)

Schumann's concerto is completely different. Almost alone of big orchestral works, it gives a feeling of radiant freshness, as if it's being improvised on the spot. The ideas seem spontaneous, fleeting, kaleidoscopic, and if there is organization, it seems simply to be a matter of the players deciding on a joint key and speed, and then following each other, picking up inspirations, stimulating each other's creativity. This is common in jazz, rock and other non-written music, and it's a feeling Schumann often gets in his solo piano works; but in the concert hall, only Chopin's piano concertos have anything like the same effect.

The work's freshness, however, is the result of much effort on Schumann's part. He wrote the first movement in 1841, in the first ardour of his marriage. It's a single, rhapsodic inspiration, in which everything grows, flower-like, from the woodwind tune at the beginning (after the first piano flourish). Four years later, Schumann set out to capture the same headiness in two more movements. The slow movement is a gentle reverie, like one of his solo piano pieces on which the orchestra is allowed to eavesdrop. The finale is like a classical music jam session, transforming all the ideas we've heard so far into headlong, effervescent dance.

HOW NOT TO PLAY SCHUMANN'S CONCERTO   Bernard Shaw describes an 1890 performance by the 'athletic' Sophie Menter. Her playing 'was like bringing a sensitive invalid into the fields on a sunshiny day and making him play football for the good of his liver. You could hear Schumann plaintively remonstrating in the orchestra, and the piano coming down on him irresistibly, echoing his words with good-natured mockery, and whirling him off in an endless race that took him clean out of himself and left him panting. Never were the quick movements finished with less regard for poor Schumann's lungs.'

NOW TRY   Schumann, Piano Sonata No. 2; Symphony No. 1, 'Spring'. Chopin, Piano Concerto No. 2. Saint-Saëns, Piano Concerto No. 2. Grieg, Piano Concerto.

SCHUMANN
'Dedication'

'Dedication' (*Widmung*) is a song of passionate devotion. 'Soul of my soul, oh thou my heart, thou art my world, my heav'n, all joy ...' The words suggest religious ecstasy, but the music is unequivocally erotic and sensual. Against a surging, swelling piano accompaniment the voice sings one of Schumann's most exquisite slow melodies. Halfway through there is a sudden key-change, and the accompaniment settles to calm chords for the words 'Thou art repose, contentment ...' But emotion begins to rise again, and soon we are surging away as at the beginning.

The poet Rückert wrote religious verse of lyric sensuality and intensity – and Schumann, in the grip of his passion for Clara Wieck, takes these qualities and heightens them to make the song an unstoppable declaration of earthly love. Art transcending art (or in this case, evoking two things at once) – Schumann, with his taste for ciphers and hidden meanings, knew exactly what he was doing.

SCHUMANN'S SONGS Schumann married Clara in 1840, after eleven years' courtship. In the first year of their marriage, he wrote almost nothing but songs, an outpouring of ecstasy so passionate and heady that some of the songs (this one, for instance) seem to have been dashed on paper in the time it took to read the words. The combination of gush and strict artistic control (the piano, for example, carries much of the 'meaning' of many songs) is typically romantic: Schumann is the Keats or Shelley of music.

DICHTERLIEBE Just as Schumann liked to organize short piano pieces into integrated, intellectually complex sets, so he did with songs. He wrote half a dozen song cycles, in which the songs all develop a single mood or make meaningful contrasts between differing moods. *Dichterliebe* ('Poet's Love') is the best known. Its sixteen songs (setting poems by Heine) describe love in all its aspects, from first glimpse through courtship to rhapsodic passion, separation – and, in a marvellous final piano page – nostalgic reverie of the happiness won and lost.

NOW TRY   After 'Dedication': Schumann, 'You're Like a Flower' ('Du bist wie eine Blume'); 'The Walnut Tree' (*Der Nussbaum*); 'The Lotus' (*Die Lotosblume*). Schubert, 'Du bist die Ruh'. Brahms, 'Gestille Sehnsucht'. After 'Dichterliebe': Schumann, 'Frauenliebe und Leben'. Schubert, 'The Maid of the Mill'. Grieg, 'Haugtussa'.

SIBELIUS
Karelia Suite

Karelia is one of the ancient names for Finland. It was also the title for a historical pageant first produced in 1893 – a mixture of heroic drama and what we would now think of as son et lumière. Sibelius's incidental music was crucial to the show, and he later published four extracts: the *Karelia* Overture (which contains many of the tunes) and this suite.

The suite, which is constantly pillaged for TV theme tunes and adverts, has three movements. It begins with an 'Intermezzo', originally written to accompany a procession of Karelians offering homage to their prince: a solemn affair of fanfares, self-important bustling and a ceremonial big tune. The second movement, 'Ballade', accompanied a scene showing a deposed medieval monarch under house arrest (or rather, castle arrest), listening to a minstrel singing of the country's glorious past – a sorrowful tune, mainly for oboe, over spread harp chords. The last movement, 'Alla marcia', representing the Karelian armies mustering for war, starts with a sprightly march tune which gathers loudness and intensity each time it's repeated, building to a sonorous, flag-waving climax.

SIBELIUS   Jean Sibelius (1865–1957), a violinist as well as a composer, won such fame for his intensely nationalist music that in 1897 he was given a state salary, for life, to continue composing. In 1931, at the height of his fame, he retired, and spent the remaining twenty-six years of his life resisting all attempts to persuade him to compose again.

SIBELIUS AND THE THEATRE   As a composer, Sibelius wore two hats. His concert works were large-scale, serious and deeply thought: choral suites, a violin concerto, a dozen heavyweight symphonic poems and seven powerful symphonies. But he also poured out lighter music of all kinds: songs, violin pieces, humoresques and other dances for small orchestra, and incidental music for a score of plays, by authors grand (Shakespeare, Strindberg, Maeterlinck) and not so grand (Paul, Lybeck, Procopé). He made suites from the best of these, and they are some of his most attractive short works: *Pelléas and Mélisande*, *Belshazzar's Feast*, *The Tempest*, *Swanwhite*.

NOW TRY   Sibelius, *Valse triste*; *King Christian II* Suite. Grieg, *Sigurd Jorsalfar* Suite. Fauré, *Masques et bergamasques*.

SIBELIUS
Finlandia

Sibelius wrote this work in 1899, and it made his name by political accident as much as by musical power. A frequent traveller, he had been abroad in Italy, and when he came home he planned a suite reflecting his feelings at seeing Finland again after a long time away. However, he returned to turmoil: the Russians had just invaded, closed down parliament and abolished free speech. A huge artistic movement of defiance began: although the concerts, exhibitions and shows never challenged the Russians directly, they asserted and celebrated Finland's Finnishness – an ironical approach which had often been used before in this much-invaded country.

Sibelius reworked his suite for one of these shows, and the final movement, a depiction of heroic struggle, made such an impression that he revised it and published it a year later as *Finlandia*. It became a symbol of Finnish resistance and identity, and brought Finland's plight to world attention, until eventually Russia relaxed its grip. Sibelius was a hero, and *Finlandia* was a national symbol.

Finlandia begins with granite grumblings from the brass, like the very earth groaning underfoot. The orchestra builds this into a picture of grandeur and vastness, and then breaks into a warlike fast section whose four-beats-to-the-bar churning keeps stumbling over inserted five-beat bars. The woodwind interrupt with a hymn-like tune – one which was, in fact, later used as a hymn, 'Be still my soul' in English – and this and the heroic struggle blend to make the work's triumphant close. Sibelius's resistance 'programme' is not explicit, but it must have been obvious to all original audiences.

SYMPHONIC POEMS   *Finlandia* is one of a dozen symphonic poems by Sibelius, which depict moods, or tell specific stories (many from the *Kalevala*: see page 183). Two in similar mood to *Finlandia* are *En Saga* ('A Saga'), a generalized picture of heroism and strife, and *Tapiola*, an overwhelming impression of the grandeur of what Sibelius in the score calls Finland's 'ancient, mysterious' forests, 'dreaming savage dreams'.

NOW TRY   Sibelius, Prelude, *The Tempest*; March from *Karelia* Suite. Tchaikovsky, *Romeo and Juliet*. Liszt, *Les Préludes*. Glinka, Overture to *Ruslan and Lyudmila*.

SIBELIUS
Symphony No. 2

Sibelius's symphonies turn the usual construction method inside out. From the time of Haydn, symphonies had been organized like formal debates. The subject was first set out, then considered in all its ramifications, and was finally restated with new conclusions in the light of the discussion. Substitute 'theme' for 'subject' and 'develop' for 'consider', and you have symphonic form.

Sibelius used an entirely different structure. His symphonies begin with unconnected wisps and fragments, splashes of music with no apparent order or relationship. The movement grows organically, and the themelets are gradually revealed as part of a coherent structure. For anyone used to nineteenth-century symphonies, this can sound chaotic; but if you relax into the music, its order soon becomes both apparent and satisfying.

Sibelius's second symphony has four movements. The first is pastoral, and its themes are so widely different that you wonder if they'll ever make a unified whole (they do). The second movement begins with aimless-seeming pluckings on double-basses and cellos, and a gloomy bassoon tune, and moves inexorably to a huge, melodramatic climax. The third movement has two fast sections framing a slow melody (beginning with nine repeated oboe notes, as if unsure what comes next). The fourth movement follows without a break, and contrasts an anguished string tune with one of those big-hearted, Technicolor melodies that carry so many Sibelius symphonies to their audience-galvanizing conclusions.

SIBELIUS'S SYMPHONIES   Each Sibelius symphony is organized in its own unique way. They range from the exuberant, Tchaikovsky-influenced No. 1 to the one-movement, brooding No. 7. For many listeners, they sum up his craggy, landscape-haunted art even better than the symphonic poems with their more specific programmes.

THE *KALEVALA*   The *Kalevala* ('Epic of Finland') is an enormous poem by Elias Lönnrot, a kind of Finnish *Odyssey*. In 23,000 lines, it tells Finland's ancient myths and legends, and is full of evocations of forests, mountains, lakes and their supernatural inhabitants. It was Sibelius's main source of inspiration. He wrote over a hundred works directly based on it, and even his 'abstract' compositions (for example the symphonies) are filled with a majestic, yearning grandeur which exactly catches the *Kalevala* mood.

NOW TRY   Sibelius, Symphony No. 1; Symphony No. 5;
En Saga. Tchaikovsky, Symphony No. 5. Harris, Symphony
No. 3.

SINGING
(except for opera)

The human voice is one of the first sounds we ever hear,
and for most people it remains one of the most agreeable.
We associate the voice with personality, with emotion –
and this gives singing an edge over most other kinds of
music. When a voice is trained, or when groups of voices
sing together, the emotional impact, as well as the sound
itself, is multiplied a thousandfold.

SOLO SINGING

In classical music, there is a close bond between solo
songs and poetry. The composer's aim is to clothe the
words in music that enhances their mood and emotion.
The musical setting lets the singer bring out the
meaning, as an actor might if he or she read the words.

When we hear folk-song arrangements by classical
composers – good examples are Haydn's or Britten's
English folk-song settings, and Copland's settings of
old American songs – the 'pull' between simple original
and sophisticated arrangement is often a major pleasure.
When a composer sets words by a major poet, the effect
can be overwhelming. The greatest song composers –
Dowland, Schubert, Fauré – seem to penetrate the heart
of the experience, so that when the song is over you feel
persuaded and satisfied, as if no more need be said.

Most composers write song accompaniments for
piano, and the accompaniments range from simple

chords supporting the melody (as in Schubert's 'Serenade' or Brahms's 'Lullaby') to complex pieces in which
the piano is an equal partner with the voice, adding
ideas and commentary which enhance the meaning of
the words. Songs of this second kind are generally
known as lieder, and are among the most satisfying of all
classical music. (For recommendations, see page 173.)

Composers sometimes use the human voice as a kind
of extra orchestral instrument, as in Nielsen's Symphony No. 3 or Górecki's Symphony No. 3 – but actual
songs with orchestra are rare, and for that reason are
especially cherishable. At the lighter end of the scale, we
recommend Canteloube's *Songs of the Auvergne* and
Mahler's *Lieder eines fahrenden Gesellen*; at the weight-
ier end we recommend Britten's Serenade for Tenor,
Horn and Strings and Richard Strauss's *Four Last Songs*.

GROUPS AND CHOIRS

Thanks chiefly to church music, this is one of the most
crowded areas of the repertoire. Church music is the
bulk of some composers' entire output – Palestrina's
Masses and Bach's Passions and cantatas spring to mind.
The range is vast, from short anthems (for example
Tomkins's 'When David Heard' and Mozart's 'Ave
verum corpus') to huge ceremonial pieces such as
Monteverdi's *Vespers* or Britten's *War Requiem*. As
starters, we recommend Allegri's sublimely beautiful
Miserere (once so revered that it was forbidden, on pain
of excommunication, for anyone to publish it or write it
down outside the Sistine Chapel choir), Dvořák's
ceremonial and delightful *Stabat mater*, Walton's
sumptuous Coronation *Te Deum* (written for the

crowning of Elizabeth II) and Fauré's austerely sensuous *Requiem*.

Secular music for small groups begins with madrigals. These are short, lyric pieces, often exploring a single mood. They were hugely popular in Renaissance times, especially in England and in Italy. Because of their shortness, they tend to be anthologized on record, so that any CD or tape will give a fair selection. Composers we recommend especially are Byrd, Morley ('April is in my Mistress' Face'), Weelkes ('O Care, Thou Wilt Despatch Me'), Gibbons ('The Silver Swan') and above all Monteverdi ('O primavera, juventú dell'anno'). In the nineteenth and twentieth centuries, several composers revived the vocal ensemble tradition: Schubert ('Song of the Spirits Over the Water') and Brahms (*Liebesliederwalzer*) wrote delightful part-songs, and we also recommend Vaughan Williams's *Five English Folk Songs* and Debussy's *Three Songs of Charles d'Orléans*.

When it comes to choirs and orchestras, there are no limits to what's available. Your taste may run to grandeur, in which case nothing can beat Beethoven's Choral Symphony, Elgar's *The Dream of Gerontius*, Tippett's *A Child of Our Time* or Bruckner's *Te Deum*. If you prefer more sprightly pieces, try Nielsen's *Springtime on Fyn* or Coleridge Taylor's tune-filled *Hiawatha*. Stir in works like Bernstein's *Chichester Psalms* (alternately heart-on-sleeve devotional and cheekily jazzy), Stravinsky's *Symphony of Psalms* (like Byzantine icons frozen in sound), and Orff's pounding, sensuous *Carmina Burana*, and you will find years of satisfying listening in this area of the repertoire alone.

FOR MORE ON SINGING   See pages 8, 40, 45, 73, 86, 139, 172, 178, 197, 217, 224.

SMETANA
The Bartered Bride Suite

The Bartered Bride was written as a comic opera, set during a village festival against a background of dancing and singing by the young people of the village; Smetana added three of these dances to the overture to make this attractive suite.

The overture is musical excitement from first note to last. The strings begin, scurrying breathlessly about, and as woodwind and brass join in the music swells to a high-spirited dance. Everything quietens down and the whole thing happens again – and again. There are half a dozen champagne overtures in the repertory, and this one is vintage. It's often performed on its own. In the suite, the dances follow: a high-stepping polka, a furiant (Bohemian folk dance alternating three-beat waltz bars with two-beat bars – ONE-ah, TWO-ah, THREE-ah, ONE-ah-ah, TWO-ah-ah – to huge hilarity on the dance floor), and a whirling, tumbling 'Dance of the Comedians' to complete the set.

THE BARTERED BRIDE   Marenka is in love with Jenik, but her parents want her to marry Vašek, one of the sons of Micha, a rich merchant. The foolish Vašek enters the inn, alarmed at having to court the woman his mother has chosen for him. Marenka, realizing that this is the man her parents have chosen for *her*, warns him that Marenka is a fickle hussy. Kecal, the marriage broker, offers Jenik 300 gold pieces to buy him off. Jenik accepts, but only on condition that Marenka marries the elder son of Micha. Jenik knows that he is that man and so will be able to marry Marenka when the plot is finally unravelled, the young couple fall into each other's arms, and Vašek, who in the meantime has fallen for the Spanish dancer in a group of travelling actors, goes off to join them as a dancing bear.

SMETANA   Bedřich Smetana (1824–84) devoted his life to expressing in music the heart and soul of his native country. He wrote operas about Bohemian history and based on Bohemian folk tales; he arranged folk dances and wrote choral and solo settings of folk texts; he seemed able, without apparent effort, to catch lilt, sun and gaiety and put them on paper. It may have been a picture-postcard view of his country and its people, but it seldom fails to lift the heart.

NOW TRY   Smetana, *Carnival in Prague*; Czech Dances (orchestral version). Dvořák, Slavonic Dances, Op. 46 (orchestral version). Weinberger, Polka and Fugue from *Schwanda the Bagpiper*.

SMETANA
'Vltava'

If you wanted to put into music the sights and sounds of your native country, it would be hard to find a simpler or more brilliant way than 'Vltava'. The Vltava is Bohemia's main river, and Smetana's brainwave was to depict its course in music, from its source in the hills to its majestic sweep past places famed in Bohemian history, with pastoral scenes and peasant dances added on the way.

The work begins with tricklings and rivulets, first on solo flute, then on flutes and clarinets, and finally on strings, swirling under a soaring melody which represents the soul of the Vltava (and hence, for Smetana, Bohemia itself). This theme gradually takes over the whole orchestra, as the river broadens and sweeps majestically on.

We pass hunters in a forest: horn-calls against the swirling river music. We pause to enjoy the polka at a peasant wedding, and the dancing lasts well into the night. In the moonlight, the river ripples as nymphs gambol in the waves. Dawn breaks, and with it comes a thunderstorm. As this subsides, the Vltava flows in full majesty past the ancient fortress of Vyšehrad, and heroic memories of Bohemia's medieval glory, married to the Vltava theme, end the piece in triumph.

MÁ VLAST 'Vltava' is the second in a set of six symphonic poems known as Má Vlast ('My country'), composed in 1874–9. Each pictures some aspect of Bohemian life or history. In order, they are: 'Vyšehrad' (high citadel of Prague), 'Vltava', 'Šárka' (picture of a legendary warrior-princess), 'From Bohemia's Woods and Fields' (pastoral scenes), 'Tábor' (stronghold of the Hussites), and 'Blaník' (mountain, mythical home of dead Bohemian warriors).

TRAGEDY AND SERENITY   While Smetana was in his early fifties, he began hearing a piercing whistle inside his head. It sounded the note high E, and the accompanying pain made music-making difficult. They were the agonizing symptoms of forthcoming deafness, and he suffered months of torment until his hearing died altogether. Then, mercifully, the pain and noise stopped as well, and he was able to recapture his youthful serenity and sunniness. *Má Vlast* was the first work written in this Indian summer.

NOW TRY Smetana, *Festival Overture*. Dvořák, *Scherzo capriccioso*. Wagner, Overture to *The Flying Dutchman*. Alfvén, Swedish Rhapsody No. 1 'Midsummer Watch'.

JOHANN STRAUSS II
The Blue Danube

A shimmer of strings, four horn notes (testing the big tune), a surge of excitement – and we're off: a dozen glorious melodies, each one topping the rest. Between each waltz and the next there are tiny bridge passages, just long enough to catch your breath and change partners before you're swept away again. When the waltz was first introduced, it was banned because the dancers held each other body to body, but the real eroticism is in the lilt of the music, a pulse which takes your heartbeat and plays games with it.

Strauss's craftsmanship doesn't extend only to tunes and rhythm. In any waltz, the problem is what to do with the 'pa-pas'. (The OOMs take care of themselves.) In *The Blue Danube*, each waltz in the sequence has differently scored 'pa-pas' – they're always there, to help the dancers, but constantly varied to delight the ear. One waltz has harp ripples, another has trills and giggles on woodwind, another plucked strings – and then, as the excitement rises, the whole brass section takes over, whooping and hallooing the music on. In authentic Viennese performances, the orchestra often holds on slightly to the OOM, stealing a little from the ensuing 'pa' – a delicious, momentary suspension of balance which tugs you along: intoxication in movement.

THE STRAUSS FAMILY   Johann Strauss II (1825–99) was the family genius, but there were a dozen Strausses in the business, in Vienna and all over Europe. They owned dance halls, hired orchestras, wrote, published and conducted the music, and in Johann's case played violin as well – *The Blue Danube* gives him a sly little solo just at the psychological moment towards the end, like an actor-manager upstaging the cast and stealing the applause. Between them, the Strausses left more than two thousand waltzes, polkas and marches, and Johann's are the best made of all.

A CHANGE OF RHYTHM *Radetzky March* (Johann I). *Pizzicato Polka* (Johann II and Josef in collaboration). *Perpetuum mobile* (Johann II). *Die Fledermaus* (Johann II – a whole operetta, crammed with tunes).

NOW TRY Johann Strauss II, *Emperor Waltz*, *Roses from the South*; *Morning Papers*; *Tales from the Vienna Woods*. Waldteufel, *Skaters' Waltz*. Lehár, *Gold and Silver Waltz*. Richard Strauss, Waltzes, *Der Rosenkavalier*.

RICHARD STRAUSS
Don Juan

Although *Don Juan* is one of the most popular of all orchestral works, writers of programme notes are often coy about its subject. Strauss was inspired by a poem written by Richard Lenau, in which the celebrated rake Don Juan asks what use is unbounded sexual energy if he can't find a single moment of genuine love. His world was ruined by a 'glimpse of eternity' in youth, and his insatiable fornication is both a quest to recapture it and also his punishment: he damns himself for what he does, even as he does it.

Strauss turned Lenau's hothouse images into a vast outpouring of musical energy. In the first bar, the orchestra seems to gather itself and leap into full-throated chase. *Don*

Juan's themes are swaggering and uncomplicated – a pouncing string tune accompanied by pulsating woodwind; an all-conquering horn tune blaring out above the orchestral texture. The 'glimpse of eternity' is a quiet oboe melody, flitting in and out of the music as if half seen or half remembered. The background music represents a carnival, during which the Don searches for his beloved and finds only easy sexual conquests.

The piece ends with an orgasmic climax followed by a fall away to silence. Commentators puzzle over this. Has the Don died? Of course he hasn't. Strauss, expert at musical descriptions of anything at all – babies being bathed, sheep being herded, bread being toasted – knows exactly what these limp bars symbolize. Don Juan's orgasmic energy, the thing he is, is all-engulfing while it lasts – and then what? Nothing – exactly the point of Lenau's poem.

STRAUSS'S SYMPHONIC POEMS *Don Juan* was the second of seven show-pieces written by Strauss in 1887–98. Each tells a story, or describes a mood, in music of great brilliance and explicitness. His subjects include the teachings of the philosopher Nietzsche (in *Also Sprach Zarathustra*, the adventures of Don Quixote (*Don Quixote*), the tricks of the medieval practical joker Till Eulenspiegel (*Till Eulenspiegel*), and his own life as creator, lover, husband and sworn enemy of critics (*Ein Heldenleben*, 'A Hero's Life').

NOW TRY Strauss, *Till Eulenspiegel*. Berlioz, Overture, *Roman Carnival*. Elgar, *Falstaff*.

RICHARD STRAUSS
Der Rosenkavalier

Strauss's previous two operas, *Salome* and *Elektra*, had been tragedies about people whose lust or suffering drove them over the edge of sanity. In 1910, wanting a change, Strauss asked his librettist Hofmannsthal for a comedy 'halfway between Mozart and Johann Strauss. Hofmannsthal obliged with *Der Rosenkavalier*, and it became his and Strauss's greatest hit.

Unlike Mozart's comedies (its inspiration), *Der Rosenkavalier* is not organized in arias, duets, trios and other 'numbers'. The music is continuous, and this means that extracts have to be torn from context and served up as 'bleeding chunks'. Strauss selected some himself, topping and tailing them for separate performance. The best-known are the Presentation of the Rose (a spoof eighteenth-century ceremony spilling into rapture as the young man and woman involved fall in love) and the final trio, in which three female voices soar and entwine above a rhapsodic orchestral accompaniment. Strauss also arranged a waltz sequence (homage to his namesake Johann Strauss II), and then stirred all these sections, and others, into a rich orchestral work, a kind of *Rosenkavalier* symphonic poem.

The extracts are good introductions to the music. But like most comic operas, *Der Rosenkavalier* benefits from being seen performed, on stage or on video.

THE STORY The Marschallin and her young lover Octavian (played by a woman) are dallying when Baron Ochs ('Ox') is announced. Ochs, a foolish, elderly rake, desires young, beautiful Sophie, and plans to court her by sending an envoy with a silver rose. The Marschallin suggests sending Octavian as messenger, and Ochs agrees. Octavian now appears, dressed as a serving-girl – he has hidden to avoid embarrassing the Marschallin – and Ochs immediately starts flirting and makes an assignation. In the next act, Octavian delivers the silver rose – and he and Sophie, predictably, fall in love. It remains only for Ochs to be discomfited and for the Marschallin to renounce Octavian in the name of love, for the opera to end with Octavian's and Sophie's declarations of undying devotion.

NOW TRY Richard Strauss, *Arabella* (similar music); Suite, *The Bourgeois Gentilhomme* (similar comedy). Mozart, *Così fan tutte*. Lehár, *Land of Smiles* (less fine music, but just as creamily Viennese).

STRAVINSKY
The Firebird Suite

The Firebird, Stravinsky's first success, was a glittering ballet produced in 1910. His suite from the music became one of the most popular pieces in the repertoire. Stravinsky once reckoned that he'd conducted it a thousand times himself, an average of once every three weeks or so for life.

The suite begins with mysterious growls from strings and brass, alternating with woodwind chirps and flutters. Then the Firebird dances in all her glory: an explosion of light and colour, as if flames and feathers had been magically transformed to sound. A gentle dance follows (in the ballet, a princess and her maids are playing in a garden). This is rudely interrupted by the dance of Kastchei the wizard, as melodramatically evil as any pantomime Demon King. Next come a cradle song and a glowing, ceremonial finale: a coronation scene where the same simple tune (starting on

solo horn) is repeated half a dozen times, each more
exultant, till the suite ends with seven 'magic' chords on
brass, and a long-held final chord.

THE FIREBIRD Prince Ivan, wandering in a forest,
captures the mysterious firebird, and frees it in exchange for
one of its glowing feathers. He finds the Princess and her
maids playing in a castle garden with the fruit of a magic
tree. But the castle belongs to the wizard Kastchei, and the
girls are prisoners. The firebird gives him a box containing
the egg which holds Kastchei's fate. Ivan fights Kastchei,
and at the climax drops the box and breaks the egg. The
wizard's spells are broken, the girls are released, and Ivan
takes the Princess home and marries her.

STRAVINSKY Igor Stravinsky (1882–1971) fell into
writing ballet music by chance, when the original composer
withdrew from writing *The Firebird*, and he was given the
commission. Its international success spurred him to write
more than twenty other original ballet scores. He composed
music of many kinds – choral works, symphonies, chamber
pieces – but he is one of the few front-rank composers to
give such attention to dance, and his ballet scores are among
his most original and enjoyable works.

NOW TRY Stravinsky, *Petrushka*; *Le Chant du rossignol*.
Holst, *The Perfect Fool*. Rimsky-Korsakov, *Sheherazade*.

STRAVINSKY
The Rite of Spring

Stravinsky wrote this work for Diaghilev's Russian Ballet in
1913. The music was so extraordinary that its first
performance caused a riot. In its day, the score was almost

unplayable, and few orchestras risked programming it. But nowadays it's a 'standard'; all orchestral players have it in their bones, and it's so well-known that it can take an effort to realize just how strange the music must once have seemed.

The ballet, set in the Stone Age, is about a girl selected to dance herself to death to appease the gods. The orchestra is huge, and the sound is by turns glittering, pounding and magically transparent. The tunes are simple, the harmony is granite-like and barbaric, as if these prehistoric times had nothing to do with our more formal age, and the rhythms are wild and percussive: in some pages of the score, each bar has a different number of beats. There are two halves, each of which begins mysteriously and quietly, and progresses through a series of short, linked dances to a climax of blood-hammering, orgiastic sound. In Disney's *Fantasia*, the animators set pictures of volcanoes erupting to this music – hardly the right images, perhaps, but an understandable response to its elemental energy.

THE RUSSIAN BALLET   Founded by Sergey Diaghilev in the 1900s, the Russian Ballet toured Europe for twenty years, with triumphant success. Diaghilev insisted on new works every season, and commissioned the finest young creative talents he could find. They included Stravinsky, Falla, Prokofiev, Picasso, Nijinsky, Karsavina, Cocteau and a dozen others – the list is a roll-call of the most imaginative minds of the twentieth century, and the ballets they made revolutionized not only dance but music, painting and clothes design, the very way people look at and think about the arts.

FIRST REACTIONS TO *THE RITE OF SPRING*   '*Le sacre du printemps*? It should be called "The Massacre of Spring"'. (*Paris critic*). 'Who wrote this fiendish *Rite of Spring*? / What right had he to write this thing? / Against our helpless ears to fling / Its crash, clash, cling, clang, bing, bang, bing!' (*Boston critic*). 'Quite simply, a revelation: the most exciting thing that ever happened to me in music.' (*Pierre Boulez*).

NOW TRY   Stravinsky, Symphony in Three Movements; *Petrushka*. Ginastera, *Panambi*. Walton, *Belshazzar's Feast*.

STRAVINSKY
Symphony of Psalms

By 1930, when Stravinsky wrote this symphony for chorus and orchestra, he had left behind the jaggedness and glitter of his earlier music (for example *The Firebird* or *The Rite of Spring* for a more formal, orderly kind of sound, a musical equivalent of the ancient Greek sculpture and classical literature he was exploring at the time. This symphony contains one passage of blare and bluster, but for the rest of the time it is calm, unhurried, as cool as iced water.

Stravinsky set the Psalms in Latin. The first movement uses words from Psalm 38: 'Hear my prayer, Lord, give ear unto my supplication'. The orchestra plays edgy, spiky music under a slow rocking chant on the voices, as if we were seeing light from a stained-glass window splintered in a prism. The second movement begins with an emotionless fugue on flutes and oboes: unflustered, poised. Then the chorus sings words from Psalm 39: 'I waited on the Lord'. The last movement begins with a heart-easing 'Alleluia', after which the orchestra has its moment of *Rite of Spring-*

ish bluster. Then the chorus sings Psalm 150, 'Praise the Lord' – at first with chattering, dancing excitement, but then, in the climax to the whole symphony, in five minutes of utter raptness, the music revolving peacefully round the same few repeated notes, an effect Stravinsky said was the musical equivalent of a Byzantine icon, taking us out of the bustle of human lives and showing us a glimpse of the stillness of eternity.

INSPIRATION IS WHERE YOU FIND IT   Stravinsky got stuck while composing the last movement of the *Symphony of Psalms*. Then one day he heard a Russian choir rehearsing, singing the same phrase of music again and again, and always making the same mistake in the same place. 'It's beautiful!' he said. 'Exactly what I need!' – and he ran back to his desk and wrote the rapt last pages of his score.

EXPLORING STRAVINSKY   From his shorter works, we recommend the orchestral *Fireworks*, the satirical piano solo *Tango*, the 'twentieth-century Brandenburg Concerto' *Dumbarton Oaks* and the jazzy *The Soldier's Tale* Suite. From his longer works, we recommend the ballets *Pulcinella* and *Apollo*, the 'opera-oratorio' *Oedipus Rex* and the Symphony in C.

NOW TRY   Stravinsky, Mass; *Requiem Canticles*. Poulenc, *Gloria*. Bernstein, *Chichester Psalms*.

STRING ORCHESTRA

String orchestras vary in size, from about nine players
(two each of first violins, second violins, violas and
cellos, plus one double-bass) to about sixty (the full string
section of a symphony orchestra). Because all the
instruments belong to the same family, they make a
particularly unified, satisfying sound, equalled only,
perhaps, by the voices of a large, well-balanced choir.

In the eighteenth century, strings were the basis of all
orchestras. Composers like Vivaldi, Bach, Handel and
Mozart wrote many works for strings alone. At the
lighter end of the repertoire, we recommend Mozart's
Eine Kleine Nachtmusik and his Divertimento K137,
and Bach's Air on the G String. Larger-scale works,
among the most sonorous pieces of the century, are
Handel's Concerto Grosso Op. 6 No. 5 and Bach's
Brandenburg Concerto No. 3.

Nineteenth-century composers tended to reserve their
deepest thoughts for full symphony orchestra. Works
written for strings were more relaxed, so that there are
few happier, more cheerful works than Rossini's String
Sonata No. 3 (one of six he wrote at twelve years old),
Grieg's *Holberg* Suite, Tchaikovsky's Serenade for
Strings (with an irresistibly lilting waltz) and Dvořák's
Serenade for Strings, a piece which is really an unending
stream of melodies, each more seductive than the last.

The twentieth century has its share of light works for
strings: we recommend Britten's Simple Symphony (a
treasure trove for advertisers), Warlock's *Capriol* Suite
(which paints twentieth-century red noses on some well-
known sixteenth-century dances) and Wirén's Serenade

for Strings, whose closing march has inspired more TV signature tunes than almost any other piece of music. But composers – particularly, for some reason, in Britain – also used the string orchestra for profundity, creating mid-length masterpieces to rival any of their works for full orchestra. You'd have to go far to beat Elgar's muscular *Introduction and Allegro*, Vaughan Williams's *Fantasia on a Theme of Thomas Tallis* or Tippett's Concerto for Double String Orchestra and ravishing *Fantasia Concertante on a Theme of Corelli* – not to mention two of the most impressive pieces of music created this century: Bartók's Music for Strings, Percussion and Celesta and Martinů's Double Concerto (1938).

OTHER WORKS FOR STRING ORCHESTRA　see pages 107, 167, 213, 226.

SULLIVAN
The Mikado

The Mikado was Sullivan's most popular piece in its day, and still is. Set in ancient Japan, it is the comic tale of a ruthless ruler (the Mikado), a reluctant executioner (Koko), a wandering minstrel (Nankipoo – needless to say, a prince in disguise) and a beautiful girl (Yum-Yum). The libretto sends up every cliché of Japanese life, and Sullivan sets it to happy-go-lucky tunes, whose only irritation is that once you remember one, you can't get it out of your head for days.

　　The opera is stuffed with favourites: the Mikado's song 'I've Got a Little List', Koko's doleful 'On a Tree by a River' ('Tit-willow'), Yum-Yum's ditty with two friends, 'Three Little Maids from School Are We', and Nankipoo's serenade 'A Wand'ring Minstrel I'. The whole thing is magnificently

silly and utterly compelling – a slight thing, perhaps, but
superbly done.

THE SAVOY OPERAS   Named after the London theatre
where they were first performed, the Savoy Operas are some
of Britain's favourite operettas. There are a dozen of them,
and the best-known are *Trial By Jury*, *The Pirates of
Penzance*, *Iolanthe*, *The Yeomen of the Guard* and *The
Gondoliers*.

SULLIVAN   Arthur Sullivan (1842–1900) yearned to be a
serious composer, Britain's Mendelssohn. Unfortunately,
his symphonies and choral works were far less popular than
the operettas he threw off in his spare time. His problem was
theatre addiction: he simply couldn't leave it alone. He
hung around in the back stalls while the shows were on, and
once absent-mindedly sang along, until an old lady turned
and snapped, 'Be quiet! I came to hear Sullivan, not you.'

GILBERT AND SULLIVAN   Calling this piece 'Sullivan's
Mikado' would have infuriated his partner W.S. Gilbert
(1836–1911). Gilbert always claimed that the Savoy Operas'
success depended on his words first and Sullivan's music
second; Sullivan took the opposite view. The fact is that
music and lyrics fit so exactly that they seem to be the work
of a single creative mind, and the creative chemistry is
astonishing, given how cordially the two men disliked each
other. Certainly neither Sullivan with other librettists, nor
Gilbert with other composers, ever reached these heights.

NOW TRY Sullivan, *The Yeomen of the Guard*. Rom-
berg, *The Student Prince*. German, *Merrie England*
(dances).

SYMPHONIES

In medieval paintings, the 'symphony' meant a group of angels playing instruments in Heaven. It was not until the eighteenth century that it came to mean music and not performers: a short piece for instruments, either introducing a vocal work or inserted in the middle, like the 'Pastoral' Symphony which introduces the shepherds watching their flocks by night in Handel's *Messiah*. At first such symphonies had one movement only, but it later became customary to have three short movements: a fast movement, a slow middle movement and a dance (usually a minuet).

HAYDN AND THE SYMPHONY

So long as symphonies were connected with vocal works, it never occurred to anyone to listen to them on their own, in concert. If you wanted to hear orchestral music, you listened to suites, not symphonies. The change began with Haydn. In his twenties, for no reason that anyone can pinpoint, he suddenly began to write independent symphonies, unconnected with any stage show or other vocal performance.

Haydn's first few symphonies are short, with three or four pint-sized movements. But in 1761 he went to work for Prince Esterházy, who had a much larger, more skilful orchestra than Haydn's previous employers. At once, Haydn began writing longer, grander symphonies. He based them on the original three-movement pattern, but expanded the scale of the first movement and added a fourth, balancing movement of similar scale.

Haydn's symphonies gradually set the pattern for other composers, and by the 1780s symphonies had displaced suites as the most popular orchestral form. Most symphonies now lasted twenty to thirty minutes, and were large-scale, serious works. You can hear the development in Haydn's own music, from the delectable but miniature Symphony No. 18, through such experiments as the 'Echo' Symphony (No. 38) or the 'Mourning' Symphony (No. 44), to his final masterpieces, the set of twelve symphonies he wrote for a London tour in the 1790s. (We recommend the 'Surprise' Symphony (No. 94), and Symphony No. 102, one of his finest.)

The only other eighteenth-century composer whose symphonies rival those of Haydn is Mozart. His first twenty or so symphonies are small-scale, but from then on they grow in size and stature, until the last half-dozen or so (Nos. 35–41), which are among the most often heard and best loved of all orchestral works.

SYMPHONIES SINCE HAYDN

After Haydn and Mozart, the next great composer to work on the symphony was Beethoven. He began by writing two standard-sized, Haydnish symphonies. But from his 'Eroica' Symphony (No. 3) onwards, he transformed the style. He wrote massive, intellectually complex symphonies, pushing them further than anyone before him. In his hands, symphonies were no longer just another kind of orchestral music: they were epics, the grandest utterances an orchestral composer could aspire to. (As a sample, we recommend what is possibly the most famous symphony ever written, Beethoven's Symphony No. 5.)

After Beethoven, the symphony kept its position at the peak of the orchestral repertoire. Dozens of composers wrote big-scale, heroic or dramatic symphonies; indeed, some composers (for example Bruckner and Mahler) wrote very little else, believing that nothing could surpass a symphony, or (as Mahler put it) that a symphony should 'contain the world'. There are a couple of dozen big nineteenth-century symphonies, and they have the same relationship to the rest of the orchestral repertoire as palaces do to ordinary houses. We recommend the symphonies of Brahms (starting with No. 2), Tchaikovsky (starting with No. 5), and Mahler (starting with No. 4).

Other composers viewed the symphony in different ways. Some, like Bizet, Borodin and Mendelssohn, wrote 'entertainment' symphonies, deliberately light and cheerful. Others, like Berlioz, wrote 'programme' symphonies, using them to tell specific stories and thinking of them as the musical equivalent of novels or plays. Good examples of the two types are Mendelssohn's 'Italian' Symphony (No. 4) and Berlioz's *Symphonie fantastique*.

In the twentieth century, the symphony fell out of fashion with some composers, who re-explored the possibilities of orchestral suites (such as Rimsky-Korsakov's *Sheherazade*, or wrote symphonic-scale works under other names (for example Debussy's 'three symphonic sketches' *La Mer* or Bartók's *Music for Strings, Percussion and Celesta*. Others did write symphonies, some of which are among the most satisfying in the form: we recommend Sibelius's Symphony No. 5, Nielsen's Symphony No. 4, Shostako-

vich's Symphony No. 10 and Walton's Symphony No. 1,
one of the finest of all symphonies of any age.

MORE ABOUT SYMPHONIES, See Pages 20, 43, 63, 78, 89,
97, 113, 116, 121, 130, 166, 169, 182, 197, 209, 228.

TCHAIKOVSKY
The Nutcracker Suite

This orchestral suite comes from Act 2 of Tchaikovsky's
ballet. In the Kingdom of Sweets, sweets come to life and
perform dances from various countries, culminating in a
swirling waltz danced by the Nutcracker Prince and the
Sugar Plum Fairy. Few ballets – and few suites – are more
often performed, recorded or cherished.

The suite begins with a gossamer-light overture. Then
follows the Dance of the Sugar Plum Fairy, a miniature
concerto for celesta (a keyboard instrument with bells
instead of strings). Three national dances follow: a
roistering Russian Dance, a melancholy Arab Dance and a
prancing Chinese Dance. The next dance, Dance of the Toy
Flutes, leads to the swaying, swirling Waltz of the Flowers.

THE NUTCRACKER   On Christmas Eve Clara dreams
that her toys come to life. The Nutcracker Prince, having
fought and defeated the Rat-king, takes her on a magic
journey to the Kingdom of Sweets, where she is transformed
into a beautiful ballerina, the Sugar Plum Fairy, and dances
the night away with her beloved prince.

TCHAIKOVSKY AND BALLET   Peter Tchaikovsky (1840–
93) was actually a composer of concert music (symphonies,
concertos, chamber works) and operas. He wrote ballets

reluctantly, and finished only three: *Swan Lake*, *The Sleeping Beauty* and *The Nutcracker*. Rather to his annoyance, each was a smash hit, and their music has headed the popularity stakes ever since.

TCHAIKOVSKY'S LONELINESS Sadly for someone whose music gave (and gives) such happiness, Tchaikovsky was a neurotic, tormented man. He was terrified by human contact (some say because he was a self-hating homosexual), and lived a solitary life composing, writing letters (sometimes up to twenty a day), playing cards and reading. When he had to meet people (which, given his fame, was often) he was abrupt and shy, and when he conducted he hunched so far down that the orchestra had to crane their necks to see him. His closest friend was Nadezhda von Meck; their relationship was conducted entirely by letter, and collapsed soon after the first and only time they met.

NOW TRY Tchaikovsky, *Swan Lake Suite*; *The Sleeping Beauty Suite*; *The Nutcracker pas de deux*. Delibes, *Coppélia* Suite. Elgar, *Wand of Youth Suite* No. 1.

TCHAIKOVSKY
1812 Overture

In 1880, a huge exhibition of Russian Art and Industry was held in Moscow, and Tchaikovsky was asked to write a new, patriotic work for it. It was to be performed out of doors, and he could use as many players as he wanted. This overture was the result: a reminder of the Russian victory over Napoleon in 1812, the dawn of the 'modern' Russian state which the Exhibition was designed to celebrate.

When Tchaikovsky wrote big pieces of this kind, he worked to a unique recipe of his own invention. He chose the main ideas he wanted to express, and gave each a musical theme. Then he ignored the original ideas, and organized the themes for their musical interest alone. This rescued the works from being simple sound-pictures, and gave them intellectual as well as pictorial power.

Four ideas underlie *1812*. A prayerful chorale (the Imperial National Anthem, later cannibalized for the hymn tune 'Moscow') symbolizes the Russian people, and the Marseillaise stands for the French. A soaring string melody and a peasant dance represent loved ones and the joys of peace. Fussy counterpoint on strings, with offbeat brass chords and cymbal crashes, gives us the fighting, with real cannon for good measure. Tchaikovsky deploys all these themes as if writing a symphony, and structures the overture as a gradual, inexorable climax, from the quiet chorale beginning to the final mortar-firing, bell-pealing victory celebration. No tape or CD really does this work justice: to be believed, it has to be seen as well as heard.

ROMEO AND JULIET Tchaikovsky used the *1812* construction method in three fantasies based on plays by his favourite author, Shakespeare: *Hamlet*, *The Tempest* and – best-known of all – *Romeo and Juliet*. In this, the main themes represent Friar Lawrence (chorale), the street-fighting between Montagues and Capulets (offbeat chords and cymbal crashes, against rushing strings), and the love of Romeo and Juliet (an ecstatic tune accompanied by sobbing horns). Hollywood composers endlessly cribbed this work for films, but music as vivid as this hardly needs cameras, lights or actors.

208   TCHAIKOVSKY

Now TRY Tchaikovsky, *Marche slave*; *Italian Caprice*.
Glinka, Overture to *Ruslan and Lyudmila*. Saint-Saëns,
Marche héroïque.

TCHAIKOVSKY
Piano Concerto No. 1

If there were a prize for the most popular concerto ever
written, the shortlist would consist of this one, Grieg's
Piano Concerto and Rachmaninov's Piano Concerto No. 2 –
and Tchaikovsky would probably win. All young virtuosos
must tackle 'Tchaik One'; until you've made your mark
with it, you haven't started.

The concerto begins with a lavish tune accompanied by
crashing chords. First the orchestra has the tune and the
piano the chords, then they change roles, and the piano
takes off on its own, celebrating its dominance. The rest of
the first movement balances a chirpy folk song and a 'big
tune' which allows both piano and orchestra to build
enormous climaxes, as if trying to outdo one another. (The
piano wins, and celebrates with a splashy cadenza.)

The second movement sandwiches a quicksilver scherzo
between two appearances of a gentle tune played first on
solo flute and then taken up and decorated by the piano.
Then, truce over, the finale brings war once more. As in the
first movement, a folk tune alternates with a soaring, film-
music-like melody. The soloist seems to shake notes out of
nowhere, scooping them up and hurling them at the
orchestra, but the big tune triumphs, and soloist and
orchestra breast the tape together with three triumphant
chords and a long-held final note.

UNPLAYABLE   Tchaikovsky wrote this concerto for
Anton Rubinstein, one of the finest pianists of the day. On
Christmas Eve 1874 he played it through to Rubinstein,
who listened in silence and then declared it unplayable, a
waste of paper. Luckily for posterity, Tchaikovsky had
already organized a public performance; otherwise he'd
have burned the score then and there. The performance was
a triumph, pianists everywhere took the work up, and in the
end even Rubinstein condescended to play it. He neither
explained nor apologized for his bizarre first reaction, and
it's impossible to guess, a century later, what the trouble
was. Certainly no other performer in the history of piano-
playing has ever spurned this work; indeed, to this day,
there are virtuosos who tour the world and make a
handsome living playing nothing else.

NOW TRY   Tchaikovsky, Violin Concerto. Grieg, Piano
Concerto. Khachaturian, Piano Concerto.

TCHAIKOVSKY
Symphony No. 6, 'Pathétique'

Tchaikovsky wrote this symphony in the last weeks of his
life, and it's hard not to feel that this is a valedictory work.
Although it's actually nothing of the kind (he planned a
seventh symphony), it still seems to sum up his feelings
about himself and his work, and he spoke of it as one of his
most personal compositions.

The subtitle means 'passionate', and emotion is the key.
The music seems to burst out of the symphonic framework,
sometimes despairing, sometimes with frantic, nervous
gaiety.

The first movement is an argument between anxiety and serenity. The anxious music is fast, blurted and fragmentary, as if the emotion were being checked as soon as uttered. The serene music is gentle and smoothly flowing: calm after storm.

In the next two movements, Tchaikovsky relaxes the tension. First comes a tuneful 'waltz' – but in five-time instead of three-time. Then follows a march, full of trumpet-calls and piccolo skirls and shrieks. Then Tchaikovsky darkens the mood again. The symphony's last movement is despairing, broken-hearted, one of the most down-beat endings ever composed – and after the wide-ranging emotional panorama of the rest of the work, it can leave you stunned.

TCHAIKOVSKY'S DEATH   The sixth symphony's sombre reputation is partly due to circumstances. It was first performed on 28 October 1893 – and nine days later, on 6 November, Tchaikovsky was dead. Scholars used to claim that he died of cholera, caused by drinking a glass of unboiled water, or that he was poisoned (no one knows by whom). But recent research has suggested that he committed suicide, after Duke Stenbok-Fermor threatened to expose him as a paedophile (something that would have brought him exile to Siberia). If this story is true, then Tchaikovsky must have known what he was planning even as he finished the symphony.

EXPLORING TCHAIKOVSKY   From his shorter works, we recommend the song 'None But the Lonely Heart', the *Andante cantabile* (orchestral version), 'Tatyana's Letter Song' (from the opera *Eugene Onegin*) and the 'Waltz of the Flowers' (from *The Nutcracker*). From his longer works, we recommend the irresistible Serenade for Strings, *Romeo and*

Juliet, Act 2 of *Swan Lake* and the exuberant Symphony No. 4.

Now TRY Tchaikovsky, Symphony No. 5. Berlioz, *Symphonie fantastique*. Mahler, Symphony No. 7.

TIPPETT
Ritual Dances

These dances, from Tippett's opera *The Midsummer Marriage*, are concert-hall favourites. They are nature-music – not rippling brooks and calling birds, but red in tooth and claw. Horns begin with mysterious, magic chords against chaotic twittering from strings and woodwind – clouds scudding, leaves torn from rain-lashed trees. A climax comes, and the storm subsides to uneasy chords as the dances begin.

The first dance, 'The Earth in Autumn', begins with a hare hopping and feeding in the grass beside a wood. A hound sniffs it out, and a chase begins before the hare breaks free and escapes, to jeering fanfares on trombones and trumpets. There is a huge burst of sunlight, then the music slows and droops as the second dance, 'The Waters in Winter', starts. A fish is motionless in a sluggish river. Suddenly it leaps to catch a fly, and an otter sees it and dives after it. They hurtle through the water, barrelling and twisting until the fish escapes and the exhausted otter climbs out on to the shore.

Another sunburst leads us to a cornfield for the third dance, 'The Air in Spring'. High in the trees, leaves tremble in the breeze. A bird hops in the field, pecking grain, and a hawk sees it and swoops. The bird escapes, but its wing is injured. Another swoop; another escape. Another; and this time, death. The music grows ever more agitated, and the fourth dance, 'Fire in Summer', begins: a picture of the blaze of noonday heat. The music gathers all the threads and themes of the earlier dances, and then winds down, closing on the mysterious horn-calls with which the work began.

TIPPETT   Michael Tippett (born 1905) found worldwide fame in his fifties, with an outstanding production and recording of *The Midsummer Marriage*. Since then he has poured out works of all kinds, as vigorous as a man half his age. No other composer in history, not even Janáček, has ever had such an astounding metamorphosis, from non-entity to one of the most renowned creative artists of the century.

NOW TRY   Tippett, *Fantasia Concertante on a Theme of Corelli*; Concerto for Double String Orchestra. Harris, Symphony No. 3. Martinů, *Frescoes of Piero della Francesca*.

VAUGHAN WILLIAMS
Fantasia on a Theme of Thomas Tallis

This work is a musical equivalent of one of those TV documentaries that show you round ancient palaces or cathedrals. Long shots give you the full perspective, but the camera also focuses on details – apse, nave, roof beams, fan vaulting – giving a sense of grandeur by juxtaposition and variety.

Vaughan Williams wrote the *Fantasia* for the 1910 Three Choirs Festival, and it was first performed in the echoing spaces of Gloucester Cathedral. It's scored for solo string quartet and two string orchestras, and is based on a hymn tune by the Tudor composer Thomas Tallis.

As the *Fantasia* begins, vast string chords fill the void; then plucked bass notes usher in Tallis's tune, played against a swirling accompaniment. Vaughan Williams then 'deconstructs' what we've heard so far, focusing on each element in turn. Solo violin and viola add a theme like a rhapsodic folk song, and the three string groups play antiphonal chords and snatches of tune. A climax carries the music to the heights, and then, after a last playing of Tallis's tune and a reminiscence of the river-like chords, a solo violin climbs like a soaring lark, and the work ends with the widespread chord with which it began.

VAUGHAN WILLIAMS   Ralph Vaughan Williams (1872–1958) was an atheist, a mystic, a lover of folk music and Renaissance counterpoint, a large, all-embracing, happy man. He wrote music of all kinds, from symphonies to film scores, from hymns to hornpipes, and is best known for the 'Englishness' of his music, and the visionary feeling it gives that there is a Truth beyond all we see or know, and that music puts us in touch with it.

NEW SOUNDS   Vaughan Williams was famous for his bemused, slightly cranky attitude to the avant-garde. He once conducted a new piece, and was then heard grumbling, 'If that's modern music, I don't like it.' (It was a piece of his own.) A student once took him a spiky composition in the very latest style, and he looked him squarely in the eye and said, 'My boy, if ever a tune does occur to you, don't hesitate to write it down.'

NOW TRY Vaughan Williams, *The Lark Ascending*; *Serenade to Music*. Tippett, *Fantasia Concertante on a Theme by Corelli*. Elgar, *Introduction and Allegro*.

VERDI
Grand March from *Aida*

It would be hard to find a grander 'grand opera' extract than this. *Aida* is set in ancient Egypt, and the Grand March accompanies the triumphal return of the Pharaoh's armies from defeating the Ethiopians. The stage fills with horses, camels, elephants, chariots, captured slaves, idols, dancing girls, princes, banners and marching soldiers. In one production, in the vast ancient Baths of Caracalla in Rome, a whole division of the Italian army was press-ganged into service. The brass blare, drums thump, percussion clashes, and hundreds of voices, plus all the strings and woodwind in the orchestra, do full justice to one of Verdi's most tonsil-trembling tunes. It's hardly subtle – the only cleverness is an unexpected change of key halfway through (after which the whole thing is repeated) – but this is the kind of spectacle Hollywood would kill for.

'CELESTE AIDA' The Grand March scene is the only brash thing about *Aida*. The rest of the opera is tender, passionate and restrained. Another extract shows what Verdi could do in quieter mode: the melting tenor love song, 'Heavenly Aida', sung by the Egyptian army commander Radames on his first entrance, and telling us (in music alone) of the depth and beauty of his and Aida's passion, but also that it's doomed.

AIDA Aida, an Ethiopian slave at the Egyptian court, loves Radames, Commander of the Guard, and he loves her. Aida's mistress, Princess Amneris, also loves Radames. The Pharaoh sends Radames to fight the Ethiopians, and he returns in triumph. Among his captives is Amonasro, Aida's father (and also, though no one in Egypt knows, the Ethiopian king). As a reward for his victory, Radames is given Amneris's hand in marriage. He meets Aida on the banks of the Nile to bid her farewell, discovers who her father is, and helps them both to escape. As a punishment, he is buried alive, and at the last moment Aida slips into his crypt, so that the last thing we hear is their voices entwined in love, and in death.

NOW TRY Verdi, 'Soldiers' Chorus' from *Il Trovatore*. Gounod, Soldiers' Chorus from *Faust*. Wagner, Prelude, *The Mastersingers*.

VERDI
La Traviata

La Traviata ('The Woman Who Strayed'), Verdi's opera based on the famous play *La dame aux camélias*, is set in Paris. Verdi contrasts the doomed passion of his hero and heroine with the carefree, heartless society in which they live. Act 1 takes place during a dance (and includes a drinking song which became one of Verdi's biggest hits); the second act includes a fancy-dress party; in the third act a carnival takes place offstage.

If the background is gaiety, the foreground blends ecstasy and sorrow. Violetta, the heroine, has her full quota of love songs ('Ah! fors' è lui'; 'Amami, Alfredo') and tragic outbursts ('Addio'), and she and the hero move from rapture to misunderstandings and back again. The score is one of Verdi's most tuneful, but even more striking is its psychological power: from the first note, you feel that you know these people, rejoice for their happiness and suffer for their pain. This intensity is Verdi's trademark, and it's seldom better done than here.

THE STORY   During a party, Violetta, a 'kept woman', falls in love with Alfredo. She is ill with TB, and hopes that he will help her to find health and happiness. But Alfredo's father begs Violetta to give up his son, since their relationship will damage the marriage prospects of Alfredo's young sister. Violetta tells Alfredo that she's found another admirer, and he denounces her. Later, he begs forgiveness, and finds her dying of her illness. All is explained, and they fall into each other's arms just before Violetta dies.

VERDI   Giuseppe Verdi (1813–1901) had his first success in 1842, and never looked back, producing a string of such masterpieces as *Rigoletto*, *Il Trovatore*, *The Masked Ball*, *The Force of Destiny*, *Don Carlos* and *Aida*. He was made a senator; letters reached him even if merely addressed 'Verdi, Italy'; he was a star. He retired at seventy-one, but half a dozen years later was persuaded to write two last operas, *Othello* and *Falstaff*. As his coffin was borne through the streets, the huge crowd sang one of his own most famous tunes, the Chorus of Hebrew Slaves from his first great hit, *Nabucco*.

NOW TRY   Verdi, *Rigoletto*; *Il Trovatore*. Puccini, *La Bohème*. Bizet, *Carmen*.

VERDI
Requiem

Verdi wrote his *Requiem* in 1874, in memory of Alessandro Manzoni. Manzoni was Italy's best-known nineteenth-century writer, a beloved and important public figure. The *Requiem*, therefore, was planned not so much as a church work – Verdi was a resolute atheist – but as a memorial piece on the largest scale.

When Verdi wrote operas, he set out not only to clothe the words in music, but to depict the underlying emotional, psychological and philosophical 'meaning' of each scene and each dramatic moment. In the *Requiem*, he did exactly the same. If the text is a prayer for mercy, he paints the devotion and repentance underlying the words. If he's describing Christ, the Lamb of God, the music is the very incarnation of ethereal purity. And naturally enough, since the main part of any requiem concerns the Day of Judgement, he gives us a full-blown, Technicolor depiction of souls crying for deliverance as the Last Trump sounds, the dead rise from their graves, the Recording Angel opens the Book of Good and Evil, devils stand by to punish the guilty, the blessed hold out their arms to welcome the innocent, and above all God, the Judge Eternal, sits enthroned in majesty.

At the time, and since, people have tut-tutted about all this, claiming that operatic explicitness has no place in church. But this *Requiem* was intended for the concert-hall, and its power lies not in religious fervour but in musical exuberance. For weeks after you hear it, it can make all other *Requiems* – and most other pieces of music – seem tame.

BRITTEN'S WAR REQUIEM   In 1961, asked to write a work for the consecration of the rebuilt Coventry Cathedral (the original was bombed in the Second World War), Benjamin Britten took Verdi's *Requiem* for inspiration, and produced one of the few big, ceremonial choral works ever to rival it. His picture of the Day of Judgement is just as explicit as Verdi's, and he brilliantly interleaves the movements of the Mass with two solo voices singing settings of First World War poems by Wilfred Owen. The effect, as prayers for deliverance are set against reminiscences of the 'horror and the pity' of war, is devastating.

NOW TRY   Verdi, *Te Deum*. Puccini, *Messa di gloria*. Berlioz, *Grande messe des morts*.

VIVALDI
'Spring' from *The Four Seasons*

The Four Seasons is played everywhere: at concerts, as background music in shops, cafés and other public places. It seems to have soaked into our very pores, so that when we hear even just a snatch of it – perhaps on a starry recording by someone like Nigel Kennedy – it is like meeting a well-loved friend.

The Four Seasons consists of twelve short pieces: four sets of three, one set for each season. A calendar in sound, it takes us through the year, with each movement painting its own sound-picture. Vivaldi thoughtfully wrote a poem for each season, to say what the music represents.

The first movement of 'Spring' uses a catchy tune which keeps coming back, like the chorus of a pop song. ('Joy at the return of spring.') The solo violin chirps and twitters like a treeful of birds. The orchestra imitates a babbling stream.

Then comes a storm, full of pattering rain from the violin, before the sky clears and celebrations begin again. The second movement ('a shepherd, dozing in a meadow') is slow and gentle. The last movement is 'a rustic dance'.

VIVALDI   Antonio Vivaldi (1678–1741) had three passions in life: music, the church and women. He became a priest when he was twenty-six, but vows of celibacy made no difference to his eye for a pretty face, and he soon found the ideal job: music master to a Venetian orphanage for girls. As a composer, he was no slouch: he could write a song in an afternoon, a concerto in a day – and people claimed that he once rushed out of church in the middle of Mass to scribble down an idea.

VIVALDI'S MUSIC   Vivaldi, expert at self-publicity, claimed to have written three thousand works. Over seven hundred survive, including four hundred and fifty concertos for solo instruments and string orchestra. The bulk are for violin, for the maestro himself, standing before his adoring orchestra, his red hair flying as he played ever flashier twiddly bits – effect before seriousness, every time.

NOW TRY   Three Vivaldi flute concertos, always known by their nicknames, 'Night', 'Storm at Sea' and 'The Goldfinch', are especially succulent, but any collection of his concertos should give similar pleasure. Handel, *The Water Music*; 'The Cuckoo and the Nightingale' (organ concerto). Bach, Brandenburg Concerto No. 2.

WAGNER
'Ride of the Valkyries' from *Die Walküre*

In Norse myth, the Valkyries were warrior-goddesses, children of Mother Earth and Odin, king of the gods. They galloped their wind-horses over battlefields, snatched the souls of dead heroes and took them to Valhalla, home of the brave, to feast for all eternity. In Wagner's opera cycle *The Ring of the Nibelungs*, one of the Valkyries, Brünnhilde, falls in love with the mortal hero Siegfried.

The 'Ride of the Valkyries' comes in the second opera of Wagner's cycle, as the Valkyries assemble on a mountain peak where only gods may tread. We hear the pounding of their horses' hooves, the storm wind of their passage, the thunder and lightning as they ride across the sky. In the opera, we also hear them singing: a wild, unearthly war cry, a fanfare which both stirs and chills the blood (in the orchestral version this is played by extra trumpets: more exciting but less unearthly).

Chilling and stirring enough in Wagner, the 'Ride of the Valkyries' gained an even more sinister context in the 1970s film *Apocalypse Now*, about the Vietnam War. Here it accompanies US helicopter gunships, swooping out of the stormy sky to spray the forests with napalm and the villagers with bullets – the majesty and terror of war summed up in an explosion of images and sound.

WAGNER'S *RING*   *The Ring of the Nibelungs*, four operas long, took Wagner twenty-six years to write. It is a huge epic, based on Norse myth, with a cast of gods, giants, dwarves, monsters and mortals, and with a plot involving magic rings, heroism, love, duty and the battle for power in the universe. To put across his story, Wagner stretched all the known possibilities of theatre, and of music: he devised new harmonies, new orchestral instruments, new ways of writing for voices, new kinds of staging and lighting, new rehearsal methods. He gathered finance and built his own theatre in Bayreuth, specially for *The Ring*. His enemies called him a madman; his supporters thought him the greatest composer in music's history; *The Ring* is still the largest, most overwhelming operatic enterprise ever put on paper.

Now TRY Wagner, 'Siegfried's Funeral March' (from *Götterdämmerung*, fourth in *The Ring* cycle); Overture to *The Flying Dutchman*. Musorgsky, *A Night on Bare Mountain*. Liszt, *Les Préludes*.

WAGNER
Prelude, *The Mastersingers*

The Mastersingers (*Die Meistersinger*) is a comic opera set in medieval times, and the prelude magnificently sets the mood. Wagner blends the main musical themes into an orchestral fantasy chuckling with counterpoint and plump with tunes.

There are two basic ideas: ceremony and love. Ceremony comes from the Mastersingers' Midsummer song contest, and Wagner uses two big march themes from the opera. The love theme is the tune of the song which wins the competition – more rhapsodic than the marches, and with more heartfelt, melting harmony. Wagner first sets out these themes, then weaves them together in a web of sound which rises to a huge climax as the overture ends with organ-like chords from brass and woodwind, acompanying helter-skelter strings.

THE STORY   The Mastersingers are preparing for their
annual song competition, and the prize is to marry Eva,
beautiful daughter of Pogner the goldsmith. A young
visitor, Walter, falls in love with Eva, and determines to
enter the contest, much to the annoyance of the town clerk
Beckmesser, who wants her for himself. Thanks to the wise
old blacksmith Hans Sachs, leader of the Mastersingers,
Beckmesser is discomforted and Walter wins the contest
and Eva's heart.

WAGNER   Richard Wagner (1813–83) was devoted to his
own genius, from adolescence onwards. He never compro-
mised, writing exactly what he wanted and mercilessly
insulting singers, players or managements who objected. He
dreamed of a 'total artwork', where everything the audience
heard, saw or felt would be guided by a single creative
personality – his own. It was megalomania, but led to some
of the most powerful of all nineteenth-century stage works:
The Flying Dutchman, *Tannhäuser*, *Lohengrin*, *The Ring
of the Nibelungs*, *Tristan and Isolde*, *The Mastersingers*,
Parsifal.

WAGNER, COSIMA AND VON BÜLOW   The power of
Wagner's personality is shown by his unorthodox wooing of
his wife, Cosima. He told Cosima, at the time happily
married to his friend von Bülow, that her true destiny was
to marry him (Wagner), and Cosima immediately left her
husband. Far from being annoyed, von Bülow agreed that
Wagner was right, was like a god on earth, and he
surrendered his wife and spent the rest of his days
conducting Wagner operas as if nothing had happened.

NOW TRY   Wagner, Overture to *Rienzi*. Strauss, *Till
Eulenspiegel*. Elgar, *Cockaigne* Overture.

WALTON
'Spitfire' Prelude and Fugue

Walton's best-known film music is for Laurence Olivier's three Shakespeare films, *Hamlet*, *Richard III* and especially *Henry V* (from which we recommend the Suite). But he also wrote music for other films, including the 1942 epic *The First of the Few*. This tells the story of R. J. Mitchell (played by Leslie Howard), a man who struggled against terminal illness to perfect the Spitfire fighter aircraft, which won the Battle of Britain for the Allies in 1940.

Walton's Prelude (the film's title music) is one of those confident march melodies which stiffen the sinews (not to mention the upper lip), brace the back and make you feel proud to be – well, human. The Fugue originally accompanied busy scenes at the Spitfire factory. Its jazzy theme grows to a full-blown orchestral piece, matching the assembly process of the aircraft. A brief interlude, on solo violin, reminds us of Mitchell's failing health, and then the bustle begins again; the big tune returns at the very end as squadrons of Spitfires fly proudly overhead.

FAÇADE   When Walton was nineteen, he wrote the music for this jazzy entertainment to words by Edith Sitwell. The whole thing is quintessentially 1920s: a flappers' giggle from start to finish. Sitwell's nonsense poems are spoken by two actors over Walton's parody waltzes, polkas, Charlestons, tarantellas and popular songs. *Façade*, intended for just one performance, caught the public imagination and has been popular ever since. It exists both in its own right and as two hilarious (and highly recommended) orchestral suites, voiceless but otherwise with every witticism and tune intact.

WALTON   William Walton (1902–83) wrote symphonies, a Shakespeare opera and three virtuoso concertos. But he was also happy to turn his hand to lighter, smaller works, and poured his flair for jazzy rhythms and glorious tunes into a series of 'entertainments', some of the jolliest chips from any composer's workshop. Typical pieces are *Portsmouth Point*, *Scapino*, *Johannesburg Festival Overture* and the pompously titled but delectable *Capriccio burlesco*.

NOW TRY   After 'Spitfire' Prelude and Fugue try Walton, *Coronation March*, *Crown Imperial*. Coates, March, *The Dambusters*. Bliss, March, *Things to Come*. After *Façade* try Walton, *Johannesburg Festival Overture*. Martinů, *La Revue de cuisine*. Ibert, *Divertissement*.

WALTON
Belshazzar's Feast

The heyday of massed choirs in Britain was the century 1850–1950 – and they were some of the first casualties of television. Every town and city boasted a choir, often several hundreds strong, and there were dozens of choral festivals and hundreds of performances each year.

Walton wrote *Belshazzar's Feast* for the Leeds Festival in 1931. He was told that he could use whatever forces he liked, so long as there were plenty of them: the massed choirs of the area (some six hundred voices), symphony orchestra, any soloists he wanted. When he asked ironically, 'Is that all?', the conductor said, 'They've got brass bands up there. Chuck in a couple of brass bands' – and Walton did.

Amazingly, since this was Walton's first big choral work, the result of all this excess was a tightly controlled,

beautifully structured masterpiece. The baritone soloist tells
the story of Belshazzar and the Writing on the Wall – no big
arias, just plain, often unaccompanied narrative. The rest of
the evening belongs to the choirs and orchestra. (Orchestras
were Walton's best suit). *Belshazzar's Feast* is built round
three enormous choral utterances: 'By the waters of
Babylon' (a lament), 'Praise ye' (an orgy) and 'Then sing
aloud' (an outpouring of triumph for Belshazzar's
downfall).

This is not a work for extracts. Its wonderful scoring
(those brass bands make all the difference), its spooky
narration (especially at the moment when the mysterious
hand writes on the wall), its sorrow and triumph engulf the
listener in a wave of sound. It lasts about half an hour, and
thirty minutes have seldom seemed so short.

THE STORY   Belshazzar, King of Babylon, has taken the
Jews into exile; he forces them to take part in orgies, and to
use the sacred Temple cups to drink toasts to his idolatrous
gods. God warns him, to no avail, then sends a hand to write
on the palace wall that he has been 'weighed in the balance
and found wanting', and will be slain. He dies, his kingdom
is divided, and the Jews sing paeans of praise to God.

NOW TRY   Walton, *Coronation Te Deum*; *Gloria*. Orff,
Carmina Burana. Bernstein, *Chichester Psalms*.

WEBERN
Five Pieces for Strings

Most composers make music by combining the elements of
music – individual notes, the gaps between them, pauses,
instrumental and vocal sound – into patterns as one makes

a painting from thousands of individual brushstrokes. Webern, by contrast, isolates each element. Single notes, sounds, silences, are put before us like exhibits pinned on a board.

This way of writing utterly changes the music's impact. In most music, emotion is created by the way the sounds are assembled; in Webern each sound's emotional charge is distinct from all the others. Feelings glint like stars in a dark sky. The effect is so concentrated that one minute of Webern can have the same kind of emotional force as ten minutes by anyone else. His works are short – a movement might last as little as fifteen seconds – and need an adjustment of concentration span. But they are extraordinarily addictive, and they have the disorienting effect, until you break the spell, of making other people's music seem bloatedly assertive.

The *Five Pieces for Strings*, written in 1909, use every known way of playing string instruments: normal bowing (in the centre of the string), bowing at the top, bowing at the bottom, plucking, tapping, with and without mute, and a dozen others. The 'cells' ('themes' seems too extravagant a description) are two or three notes long, and are played right way up, upside down, backwards, or strung in sequence like beads on a necklace. Speed, loudness and softness never settle but flash past our ears.

In all Webern's works he aimed to create what he called *Klangfarbenmelodie* ('sound-colour tunes'). The effect is like leaves in sunshine or drops in a waterfall: the pattern may only gradually become apparent, but it's none the less there.

WEBERN   Anton Webern (1883–1945) worked as conductor and music adviser to Austrian Radio. He never expected his works to be successful in his lifetime, but after his death (he was accidentally shot by a GI on the last day of the Second World War) he became a posthumous guru to hundreds of composers, one of this century's most influential musical minds.

NOW TRY   Webern, *Six Pieces for Orchestra*; *Five Pieces for Orchestra*. Stravinsky, *Variations in Memoriam Aldous Huxley*. Boulez, *Éclat*.

... AND DON'T FORGET ...

BEETHOVEN, Sonata No. 8, Op. 13, 'Pathétique'   Three movements: passion, lyricism, dazzle. One of the top piano pops.

BRITTEN, *Ceremony of Carols*   Medieval carol-words, given diamond-bright settings for boys' choir and harp.

CHOPIN, Sonata No. 3   Not really a sonata, more a suite of four characteristic Chopin movements: heroic opening, headlong scherzo, nocturne and quicksilver finale.

GLINKA, Overture to *Ruslan and Lyudmila*   Glinka's opera crams in knights, damsels, wizards, enchanted castles – every fairy-tale ingredient you've ever heard of. The overture is all swirl and swagger, heroic endeavour pinned down in sound.

MENDELSSOHN, Octet   Written at sixteen, a stunning combination of boyish vigour and mature genius. 'Just look what I can do!'

MOZART, Symphony No. 29   If Mozart is the supreme desert-island composer (and we think he is), this is one of the most cherishable of all his works.

TCHAIKOVSKY, Violin Concerto   Heroic concerto fireworks meet sumptuous tunes and sparkling orchestral effects.

WAGNER, Prelude and Liebestod from *Tristan and Isolde*   The opera tells of high-powered, doomed love. The Prelude sets the emotional scene, and the *Liebestod* is Isolde's passionate farewell to Tristan, and to life.

KEYWORDS

Aria Aria (Italian, 'air') was originally one of many alternative words for 'tune'. When opera was invented in the early seventeenth century, it was used to mean a big solo song, the operatic equivalent of a dramatic soliloquy. It still keeps this meaning. Some arias (for example 'Voi che sapete'; see page 119) are free-standing, independent of the music that surrounds them. Others (for example 'Nessun dorma': see page 145) are part of a continuous texture, and although they're popular they lose some of their effect if the context is removed.

Authentic movement This means playing music so that it sounds as nearly as possible the way the composer and original audiences heard it. The authentic movement is particularly strong in pre-1850s music: performers seek to strip away the changes brought by modern instruments and modern playing styles. Today's instruments are generally larger and more powerful; we use bigger orchestras and choirs; we tend to perform music more slowly than people used to do. Authentic performers reverse these trends.

Baroque Originally an architectural term (for extravagantly ornamental buildings of the seventeenth century), this word came into music to mean composers and works of the century 1650–1750. Vivaldi, Bach, Handel and Telemann are the main Baroque composers mentioned in this book.

Canon Two people can sing a tune simultaneously, sounding each note at the same time as one another. If, instead, one singer starts the tune alone, and the other begins it a few notes later – and if the tune fits with itself from start to finish – the result is a canon.

Continuo Accompanying instruments in seventeenth and eighteenth century music. The continuo consisted of a bass instrument (usually bass viol or bassoon) and a harmony instrument (usually harpsichord, organ or lute).

Counterpoint   In much music, one leading voice or instrument is accompanied by the others: the music is 'vertical'. In counterpoint, each voice or instrument has its own independent line of music, and the lines intertwine and blend to make the effect. The music is 'horizontal'.

Finale   Last movement.

Folk Music   Modern 'folk' is popular music in which songs are written in reaction to contemporary events and situations. To classical musicians, however, 'folk music' means 'music of the people': improvised songs and dances, often centuries old, the opposite of the 'art music' written by professional composers.

Fugue   The fugue (from Italian *fuga*, 'flight') is an intellectual descendant of the canon. Voices or instruments enter one after another, in ordered sequence. Each begins with the same musical 'subject' as all the others, then continues differently before returning to the subject. For composers of counterpoint, there are few more demanding or satisfying musical forms.

Harmony   Harmony (Greek, 'agreement'), in music, means groups of notes that fit together to make pleasing combinations of sound. You can play several notes simultaneously on a piano, for example, to make a 'harmonious' sound. Composers organize the balance of harmony and disharmony in their music to give an effect like that of light and shade in painting.

Improvise   To make music up as you play it.

Lieder   *Lieder* is simply German for 'songs'. But when Schubert's songs were first published, the volumes were given this title, and performers and composers took it to mean something more serious, more complex, than simple 'songs'. The idea grew that *Lieder* were 'art songs', where the music extended and deepened the words' emotional meaning. Other composers took up the style, and *Lieder* became a favourite concert form, with some composers and performers specializing in nothing else.

Movement   Complete section of a longer work such as sonata, symphony or suite. Movements are generally self-contained, but enhance each other's effect, so that the complete work is more than the sum of all its movements.

Orchestration   Arranging music for orchestra.

Rondo   A piece of music in which the same section comes round several times, alternating with others in contrasting styles. If we label each section with a letter of the alphabet, calling the main section A, then standard rondo form is A-B-A-C-A-D-A. Rondos are often used as the last movements of symphonies, sonatas and other large-scale works.

Scherzo   Scherzo (Italian, 'joke') is the name musicians give to a quick, indeed often tumultuous, movement in a sonata or symphony. Most scherzos are in three-time.

Scoring   Musician's slang for orchestration.

Theme   A sequence of notes forming the basis of a musical movement. Some themes are long enough to be thought of as 'tunes'; but many composers (Bach and Beethoven, for example) wrote themes of as few as two or three notes, and wove them into enormous musical textures.

INDEX